CHARLES TOWERS-CLARK

WEIRD GROUP PUBLISHING, UK

www.weirdceo.com

Contents

About the author

INTRODUCTION   *1*

1. THE NEED TO BE WEIRD   *9*
   a) The need for change   10
       i.   Technological challenges   11
       ii.   Business challenges   12
       iii. Social challenges   16
       iv.   Educational challenges   18
   b) Being WEIRD   21
       i.   Wisdom   23
       ii.   Emotional Intelligence   24
       iii. Initiative   26
       iv.   Responsibility   27
       v.   Development (Self)   29
       vi.   Circling through WEIRD   31

2. TECHNOLOGICAL CHANGE   *33*
   a) From the first to the fourth Industrial Revolution   34
   b) Disruptive technologies   36
   c) Computers, Big Data & IoT   41
   d) Machine Learning & Deep Learning   49
   e) The effect of Automation   56
   f) The Danger of Specialising   61

3. BUSINESS CHANGE   *63*
   a) Self-Management   64
   b) Communication & Scalability   71

c) Competition   74

4. *SOCIAL CHANGE*   **77**
     a) The purpose of work and life   78
     b) Who owns the data in a data driven world?   82
     c) The litigation & regulation paradox   86
     d) Social implications of automation   93
     e) Universal Basic Income   97

5. *EDUCATIONAL CHANGE*   **103**
     a) Changing our educational system   104
         i. Project based learning   105
         ii. Personalised learning   107
         iii. Teaching emotional intelligence   109

6. *THE THEORY OF WEIRD*   **111**
     a) Change starts at the top   112
     b) Focusing on the things that you can change   115
     c) In and Out   116
         i. Recruitment process   116
         ii. Conflict   117
         iii. Dismissal   118
     d) Performance & Rewards   120
         i. Transparency of salaries   120
         ii. Deciding own salaries   121
         iii. Evaluation and appraisals   122
     e) Team Working   124
         i. Seating plans   124
         ii. Avoiding stars and egos   125
         iii. Organisation and teams   126
     f) Ownership and Responsibility   129

	i.	Transparency and education of company financial information	129
	ii.	Company policies (e.g holidays, expenses, flexi-hours, training)	131
	iii.	Roles vs tasks	134
	iv.	Decisions	135
	v.	Strategy	137
	vi.	Ownership of the business	139
g)	Change, reinforcement and getting everybody on Board		143
h)	Women and WEIRD		145

7. DESTROYING THE OLD POD WORLD — **147**

a)	The company – Pod Group	148
b)	Money is a non-motivator (week 2)	149
c)	Creating the perfect organisation (optimistically) – (week 4)	150
d)	Presenting to the team, give no answers – (week 5)	153
e)	Best if the boss leaves – (week 6)	154
f)	People hate change – (week 7)	155
g)	Moving to stage two of the change process – (week 8)	157
h)	The initial proposals – (week 9)	160
i)	First draft proposal – (week 10)	161
j)	Accepting the cold shoulder – (week 11)	162
k)	Confronting the real problem – (week 12)	163

8. BUILDING THE WEIRD POD WORLD — **165**

a)	Light at the end of the tunnel – (week 13)	166
b)	Getting to a workable solution – (week 14 & 15)	167
c)	Explaining reinvestment – (week 16)	169
d)	Showing salaries – (week 17)	170
e)	Mangers – (week 20)	171
f)	The first evaluation – (week 21)	172

g)   The first chosen salaries – (week 22)   174
h)   Teal to WEIRD and on – (week 26)   175

9.   **ACTING WEIRD**   **177**
a)   POD and WEIRD   178
b)   Authentically WEIRD   181
c)   Luck and preparation   184
d)   Culture and values   187
e)   Learning to trust   189
f)   Treat everybody as an owner and CEO   192

CONCLUSION   **195**

Dedication   200
Acknowledgements   201
References   202

About the author

Charles Towers-Clark, Group CEO of Pod Group, is an entrepreneur, international lecturer and Forbes.com contributor. Charles transformed Pod Group into a WEIRD organisation to maximise the decision-making power of each person within the company – whilst minimising his own.

Before founding Pod Group in 1999, he lived and worked in Russia and Central Asia and is now based in Cambridge, UK. Based on his experiences of establishing, running and re-inventing Pod Group, he provides advice to CEOs worldwide.

INTRODUCTION

"What we fear of doing most is usually what we most need to do"
Ralph Waldo Emerson

On a recent flight in Canada, I was jolted out of a reverie during the mandatory safety briefing by the flight attendant who informed us that, although we were in the air, if we weren't happy with the service we were free to exit the plane at any time.

As I was researching for this book at the time, it made me wonder how replaceable the job of a flight attendant is.

Imagine a robot handing out food and drinks, telling people when to sit down, dealing with frayed nerves or being able to handle an emergency. To create a robot with the necessary dexterity as well as the compassion of a human being would be incredibly difficult. So, flight attendants are probably safe in their job for a long while. Pilots on the other hand may have cause for concern – if we have autonomous cars, it is only a question of time before we have passenger planes flown by computer (the military already uses pilotless planes).

Unfortunately, pilots will not be the only ones losing their jobs. The speed of technological advancement due to Artificial Intelligence and more especially Machine Learning will create a major upheaval in the number of jobs available, the way we work and the type of work that we do.

Any task that consists of a series of processes will, in the near future, be automated by a computer or robot. Not all tasks within each job can be processed, but the speed of automation (and therefore a reduced requirement for human involvement) will grow exponentially. This isn't something that will happen at some undetermined point in the future – it is already happening. Within the next five to fifteen years, a huge number of jobs will be destroyed. Many argue that, as with previous industrial revolutions, others will appear but finding alternative employment for millions of jobs that have been replaced by computers and robots will be impossible until we fundamentally change the way we think of work.

An interesting documentary entitled *7UP*, which charts a group of children from all social classes every seven years until they are fifty-six years old, showed how their lives changed over those years and how that compared to expectations. Most participants followed the course expected of them. However, one pointed out that, although he had followed the journey envisaged by his parents when he was seven years old, the future of university choices and careers is far more uncertain and impossible to predict for today's seven-year-olds. This change in personal uncertainty is also reflected in the business world. The necessity to scale and the speed with which new competition evolves have intensified such that we cannot continue to run our companies in a traditional manner.

These are not the only problems that we will face in the next fifteen years. We have (unwittingly) created the perfect sociological storm, including the social havoc that Artificial Intelligence will create, an increasing need for instant gratification, and an education and training system that is not preparing us for the future of work.

At my company, Pod Group, we generally employ young people, train them and promote internally where possible. This hasn't been without its challenges. At the risk of making some gross over-generalisations, candidates from the millennial generation have been told that they should go to university on the promise of a great job at the end. Instead, they got the 2008 financial crisis, unemployment, student loans and deflated expectations. They were brought up by baby boomers and educated for a world that no longer exists. If we are to believe the stereotype, they represent a generation that feels entitled (through no fault of their own) and is afraid of making decisions without the approval of others.

Social media is either the symptom or the disease of this need for constant approval. Either way, the need to be liked (and the dopamine rush that accompanies each like[i]), combined with the feeling of potentially missing out if you are not online at all times, has created a society which expects instant gratification in many aspects of life. Unfortunately, work doesn't often provide a constant stream of gratification; satisfaction possibly, but not gratification. This expectation is, however, driving positive changes in the workplace.

Is it possible to create an environment where enjoyment becomes the overriding characteristic of work?

As a new generation appears, so does a new way of working. Older[ii] millennials' greater sense of entitlement and expectation[iii] has driven a new approach to gaining a better working life. Younger millennials value soft benefits such as company culture, social responsibility and flexible working. For many, money is a secondary issue. Companies ignore these benefits at their peril as the best employees will go elsewhere. This is why so many talented graduates prefer to work in a start-up; because founders often have soft benefits at the core of the business.

However, are these soft benefits ingrained or just on the surface? At a meet-up in Cambridge, UK, a city full of entrepreneurs and start-up companies, I expressed the view that CEOs in Cambridge would be very good at using soft skills to run their companies. Several people disagreed, pointing out that most founders have good intentions when their businesses are in start-up mode. However, once the company is selling products and creating revenue, the CEOs and managers revert to management by diktat. This is especially true when investors' goals are focused on the financial success of the company, soft benefits are not regarded as core to the business, and the company lives and dies by its financial success alone.

Strangely, a modern-day contract of employment is similar to a contract of employment in Roman times (assuming that you weren't a slave).[iv] In both cases, the contract outlines an exchange of time for money. What was missing in Roman times, and is still missing, is the employer's commitment to provide satisfaction to the employee. Contracts state that the employee has to undertake their job responsibly, but they do not designate ownership, authority or responsibility to the employee. I am not referring to legal responsibility, but rather personal responsibility to own the task or role that needs to be accomplished. Only when employers and employees understand the correlation between satisfaction and ownership will it be possible to replace legal contracts, that focus on the exchange of time for money, with contracts of mutual benefit that will facilitate employee engagement. Ironically, employment law in most jurisdictions is making this type of shift increasingly difficult.

Futurists sometimes argue that the world would be a better place if people could have a life of leisure and computers and robots did all the work.[v] However, for many of us, the salary we earn, the job we do and our job title reflect our value. Therefore, the act of work (whether paid or voluntary) provides a measure of our self-worth. If we remove a purpose for being – whether that is bringing up a child or being part of a company – how do we encourage the feeling of responsibility and ownership?

As we will see greater technological changes over the next fifteen years than have been seen in any other fifteen-year period, we need to change the way that we think and work. Part of that change may include the introduction of Universal Basic Income. This form of guaranteed income breaks down the assumption that all people should work and offers citizens a level of choice as to how they want to live – on the presumption that people are able to take responsibility and ownership of their own lives. However, Universal Basic Income (as with government social security today) relies on the payment of taxes, including income taxes – and so there needs to be a working class.

On a global level, we must look at how we educate children and train adults to take ownership of their lives so that they can enjoy, and are encouraged to become part of, that working class. I belong to a multi-cultural family and a multi-cultural workplace and I have had the opportunity to experience various educational systems in different countries in Europe. While there is no question that change is happening in many schools, we are still educationally spoon-feeding children and the input today seems very far away from the output required tomorrow. We need a radical change in the way that schools inspire and grow children. In the future, we will need individuals who can think for themselves, motivate themselves and resolve problems for themselves. In general, however, our educational system does not provide the training to accomplish this. Much of the solution lies in the need to encourage Emotional Intelligence. According to a study by TalentSmart, Emotional Intelligence influences 57% of success across every type of job and plays the biggest role in performance when compared to 33 other workplace skills.[vi] Many schools are starting to use Social and Emotional Learning (SEL), but certainly in the United States where SEL preparation of teachers in a recent study has been shown to be low – there is a long way to go.[vii] This should be a major focus of schools. A 2015 report on the economic value of SEL calculated a cost-benefit ratio of eleven to one.[viii] Investment in Emotional Intelligence at school not only improves academic results but also reduces negative behaviour and emotional stress. This improvement in attitudes, leading to greater commitment and motivation, is required within our children today at school to help them tomorrow at work.

Companies need to evolve continuously in order to stay relevant. Some of the business and social changes covered in this book would have been required even without the effect of Artificial Intelligence. However, Artificial Intelligence adds another dimension of complexity and urgency as roles will become redundant and technology takes over. To overcome this, employees need to utilise those characteristics that cannot be replicated easily by computers. Passing more responsibility and ownership to employees promotes these characteristics and, by fostering company ownership, a secondary advantage arises – the ability to make use of each and every brain rather than resting power solely in a CEO.

In our company, Pod Group, we have started a change process using various tools to encourage employees to take ownership of their jobs and indeed of the company as a whole. As a technology company, we are both threatened and excited by the possibilities of Artificial Intelligence and know that we need to change. To manage this, we focused on the following characteristics:

Wisdom
Emotional Intelligence
Initiative
Responsibility
Development (Self)

and brought it into, what we call, the WEIRD methodology. We all work where and when we like, we speak nine different languages (sometimes in one conversation) and we choose our own salaries. But we don't drop the ball and we feel responsible for our work. Some of us like to talk to machines, some to people; some know our partners, some our platforms; but we all control our own destiny. This is how WEIRD works – oddly enough, if you let people choose how to do their work, they actually want to do it.

By encouraging employees to act as owners, not only can the changes that will be forced by Artificial Intelligence be used to positive effect, but the need for a CEO can be reduced. The ultimate success of a company practising WEIRD is to render most of the role of the CEO redundant.

I'm trying!

Chapter 1

THE NEED TO BE WEIRD

"If everyone is thinking alike, then somebody isn't thinking."
George S. Patton – US General

A) THE NEED FOR CHANGE

"Change before you have to."
Jack Welch – Ex-Chairman General Electric

09:27 4th May 2017

I walked into the office – everybody went quiet. Not the contemplative silence of thoughtful discussion; nor the uncomfortable 'we've run out of things to say' silence, but rather an icy silence which says: 'We don't like you at the moment and we definitely don't like what you have done.'

This is going to be a fun day.

What had led to this less than balmy reception was that I had taken a profitable company, with great people and really good employee interaction and said, "We need to change – I am going to take you all out of your comfort zone and make you all – well – really uncomfortable".

So why did I do it?

For two reasons – one personal, one professional. First the personal:

Some years ago, I grew a company with 120 people across 7 offices. I was young and inexperienced and didn't know how to delegate. As a result, I spent all my time on personnel issues and worked 16 hours a day. When I started Pod Group, my original intention was to employ only myself and one or two others. However, as an entrepreneur I couldn't resist the temptation to grow – and I came to realise that, in order to avoid being overworked, I needed to manage the company in a different way.

One of my sources of inspiration was Ricardo Semler of Semco who, over a period of ten years, managed to avoid making a single professional decision. His colleagues threw a celebratory party to mark this event (granted he had been removed from the CEO position by the employees, even though he is the major shareholder of the company). I realised this was a measure of success, how few decisions need to be made by the CEO and managers.

Sustainable businesses must be structured such that change takes place naturally - without the intervention of the CEO. Very few companies last more than a hundred years. In fact 50% last less than five years and 70% are bankrupt within ten years.[i]

The challenges facing businesses today are not getting easier, and that is before we consider the effect of Artificial Intelligence.

Professionally, there are four reasons for changing our approach to work: technology, business, social issues and education.

1) Technological Challenges

In order to survive and prosper in a machine-dominated world, we need to change our mentality towards work. Part of the reason for this is that technology will change at an exponential rate. The blogger Tim Urban explains the effect of exponential change:[ii]

> "It takes decades for the first AI system to reach low-level general intelligence, but it finally happens. A computer is able to understand the world around it as well as a human four-year-old. Suddenly, within an hour of hitting that milestone, the system pumps out the grand theory of physics that unifies general relativity and quantum mechanics, something no human has been able to definitively do. Ninety minutes after that, the AI has become an ASI [Artificial Super Intelligence], 170,000 times more intelligent than a human".

The changes brought about by Artificial Intelligence are different to the employment changes of previous Industrial Revolutions when only manual jobs were replaced. Over the coming years, computers will take over many tasks of an intellectual nature (eg legal work)[iii] and society will need more creative, rather than mundane, jobs.

There is a potential for mass unemployment – due to a combination of technology and the inability of people to make cultural changes at the same pace as the introduction of new technology.

A survey conducted by Quartz in 2017 explained why human complacency is a concern.[iv] This found that 90% of respondents believed that up to half of all jobs would be lost to automation within five years, but 91% thought that there was no risk to their own job.

The implications of the technological changes that are taking place can be summarised as follows:

Any job that can be defined within a process can, and probably will, be replaced by a computer. This will destroy more jobs than can be created within a short period of time in today's culture and environment;

To avoid this, we need to change the way that we work so that we can embrace and work alongside computers to replace the jobs that will be lost.

2) Business Challenges

As a race we are very good at making incremental improvements but not so good at dealing with core issues. This is especially true in business, where livelihoods, reputations and pride are at stake. Hierarchies, communication and scalability are at the core of each business – and often require fundamental rather than incremental changes.

Hierarchies

Hierarchical organisations have existed for as long as we have lived and worked in groups.

However, within the last generation or two, it has become clear that hierarchies are not necessarily the most effective structure for optimising returns. Furthermore, employees are no longer willing to follow orders blindly for the benefit of their bosses or shareholders.

From birth we are programmed to listen and obey. At school we are taught within a framework which limits initiative, and most of us have worked in organisations where the structure is deemed to be more important than the output.

Despite the disadvantages of this structure, it is difficult to dismantle as we have been trained to listen to figures of authority. I am constantly reminding managers not to make decisions on behalf of their colleagues – and encouraging employees to make decisions for themselves rather than relying on their managers to do so.

A dictatorship is one form of hierarchy and has advantages when the dictator is very good at his job. For example, Peter the Great made Russia a global power (though he caused many to die in the process). However, if the dictator makes bad decisions (for example Hitler) – the country, or organisation, is likely to fail. Many companies are, in effect, dictatorships – with the corresponding rise and fall of the company depending upon the CEO's abilities. Ironically, in 99.9% of companies, the group of people with the best understanding of the effectiveness of the CEO has no say in his or her appointment – namely the employees.

Likewise, employees are rarely willing, or in a position, to express a critical opinion to a boss on whose goodwill their jobs depend. One of the reasons I have generally tried to avoid reporting to a boss is that I find it very difficult to ensure that I am doing my job as best I can as well as doing what my boss wants me to do. Whilst these two objectives should be the same, the natural tendency is to prioritise tasks expected by the boss, even if this not to the benefit of the company. I admire employees who, working on limited information, manage to understand what their boss expects. However, I am sure this is one of the key causes of work stress.

Many bosses assume (wrongly) that they understand the job better than their underlings, resulting in a strong possibility that their decisions have little relation to the problems being addressed.

Employees in hierarchical organisations are not encouraged to collaborate with others with whom they do not share a direct report. This motivates individuals to put their own agenda before that of their team or organisation. Pushing a selfish agenda may allow them to climb up the hierarchy and gain more power, money and status; but it also creates a natural tendency for competition between colleagues and withholding of information – to the detriment of the company. This is particularly evident during the allocation of budgets – a hotspot for rivalry within hierarchical organisations.

However, the greatest disadvantage of hierarchical organisations is slow communication leading to delayed and disjointed decision making.

Communication and Scalability

Another disadvantage of hierarchical organisations is that decision making is laborious due to the need to follow a chain of command. This also has a detrimental effect on the efficacy of communication.

I am not advocating that we should all take up smoking but a friend of mine, working in a large hierarchical organisation, pointed out that he could get things done much quicker than others because, when he had a problem, he would go outside and ask for help from his smoking buddies who had created a communication channel that bypassed the hierarchical structure. This example provides evidence that communication, and therefore productivity, are optimised naturally in small groups.

The effect of productivity per person falling when more people are added to a team is known as the Ringelmann effect. Ringelmann measured the force pulled by an individual on a rope and continued to measure as more people were added. With the addition of each new person, the pull force (or efficiency) of the previous recipients dropped by about 6%. So, with eight people, each person was only exerting 50% of the force compared to when they were on their own.

The Ringelmann effect is mostly linear; adding new people into a team, depending upon their role, character, experience and other factors, could have a greater or lesser effect – but for sure the efficiency of the group will diminish.

Leaving aside the need to employ more people to overcome the Ringelmann effect, hierarchical organisations can theoretically scale to an infinite size.

Within organisations with a flatter structure, including Pod Group, a scalability problem exists as there is often no structure to support infinite growth. How do such companies maintain their level of service whilst taking on more customers?

Artificial Intelligence will provide part of the answer. The other part is to organise companies in such a way that scaling comes naturally.

However, this is often stifled during the development of new organisations. In a start-up environment, with less than ten people involved, everybody knows what's going on. As the company scales, there is a natural tendency to create silos, with a 'them and us' mentality which pushes people to become 'specialists' in their area – and a resistance to any perceived interference with that specialism. There is no easy way to avoid this but organisational changes discussed in Chapter 3 can be implemented to scale infinitely within flat organisations.

While addressing the business challenges relating to scalability, communication and the effects of Artificial Intelligence, social challenges also need to be overcome.

3) Social Challenges

The way that we work has changed more in the last 30 years than in the previous 200 years. One of the consequences is that, in developed economies, we have a level of choice that would have been inconceivable to our forefathers. However, with choice comes uncertainty.

The American psychologist Barry Schwartz studied the effects of too much choice in his book, *The Paradox of Choice* and in a TED talk[v]. Schwartz' premise was fairly simple – too much choice is a bad thing.

Various studies have shown that too much choice results in paralysis of decision making[vi]. Some supermarket chains, such as CostCo or Aldi, have understood this and deliberately offer fewer choices, but the paralysis of choice runs through everything in our lives. Schwartz quotes research carried out on investment decisions made through employee schemes at Vanguard. For each additional 10 funds offered to employees, those who joined a pension scheme dropped by 2% (due to indecision) – despite the fact that employees would get free matching funding from their employers.

Too much choice leads people to question their decisions when unrealistic expectations of perfection result in disappointment.

According to Schwartz, the secret to happiness is having low expectations. Much has been written about the high expectations of millennials but there is a surprising difference between the expectations of older versus younger millennials. Older millennials have higher expectations within many aspects of their life. This has led to some positive changes in the workplace where employers have needed to change their attitude towards employees in order to attract and retain millennials. The most important of these (in my opinion) is the move to self-management which allows employees greater choice over how they work.

With each new generation come new ideas, enthusiasm and approaches. These will be required as there is no single magic wand to solve the social problems of the world. In fact, as the world becomes more intertwined, it is increasingly necessary to take a multi-pronged approach to social issues. For example, assisting a village in a developing country requires intervention at multiple levels, including irrigation, sanitation, health, education and access to markets. However, many of our social institutions (for example the National Health Service or the prison service) were created in an industrial age and designed to relieve the symptoms rather than the cause of a problem.

Current generations, accustomed to disruptive technologies, are beginning to think about restructuring rather than just tinkering at the edges of existing systems. The changes quoted below by Indy Johar, founder of Dark Matter Labs, require this type of mindset:[vii]

> *"This future of social innovation requires us to also recognise change in this world cannot be designed as a strategy written for one organisation but has to consist of the investment in growing a movement of change, or shared intent, a mission which is an open invitation to take part and innovate together; a shared language and understanding of interdependent issues; and the distributed collective intelligence and agency of a movement. This is a future which fundamentally asks us to rewrite the models of change—from hard power to soft power, from command and control to protocols, mutual accountability, investment & system leadership".*

There is of course a flip side to this creation of interdependence – the generation, with or without our knowledge, of data. Data are already being used to make decisions for us, to guide our buying choices, our medical choices, our reading choices – in fact data are becoming increasingly important in our lives.

An example of this is health data which bizarrely, despite being about our bodies, do not necessarily belong to us. In the US, with the exception of New Hampshire, no state specifies that individuals own their health data.[viii] So, who does? Generally, the person who authored the data owns the data. This applies to data captured as a result of a hospital visit as much as to a website visit. As data are becoming the new gold, I will explore who owns the data about ourselves and to what extent we are willing to let others use that information to increase our perceived happiness or satisfaction.

An obvious, though hard to implement, solution is to add much higher levels of regulation to data control. Within Europe in 2018, new legislation was enacted to try and protect consumers against abuse of their personal data. However, the need for legislation goes beyond protecting data – and it can go too far. I used to live in Russia where the natural inclination (a throwback to Soviet times) is bureaucracy for its own sake. Even now, each apartment building has its own authority and it is necessary to deal with that bureaucrat to get a sink mended.[ix] Luckily, in Western countries, on the whole bureaucracy is less intrusive.

However, we will need some legislation around Artificial Intelligence. Various business and other leaders are calling for regulation due to the potentially detrimental ways that it could be used. The reverse argument is the danger of stifling innovation both of which will be explored later.

The fastest disruption of jobs that we will ever have seen will be caused by Artificial Intelligence. The social implications of this could change our view on employment, such that we need to look seriously at such alternatives as Universal Basic Income.

4) Educational Challenges

It is interesting that the most popular TED talk prior to publication of this book was by Ken Robinson entitled 'Do schools kill creativity? It has been listened to over fifty million times and, although very humorous, clearly resonates around the world.

The summary in his own words is[x]:

> *"I believe our only hope for the future is to adopt a new conception of human ecology, one in which we start to reconstitute our*

conception of the richness of human capacity. Our education system has mined our minds in the way that we strip-mine the earth: for a particular commodity. And for the future, it won't serve us. We have to rethink the fundamental principles on which we're educating our children".

It is surprising that educational systems around the world are not more active in re-thinking these fundamental principles. After all, at least fifty million people have an interest in Ken Robinson's viewpoint.

Many progressive schools that are trying new ways of education have either removed themselves from the need to follow the National Curriculum or have spent much time trying to work out how to adjust the way they educate to meet the minimum requirements of the curriculum whilst keeping to their core beliefs – although these are often contradictory.

An example is given in Frederic Laloux's book *Reinventing Organisations*[xi]. He interviewed staff and students at a secondary school in Berlin called ESBZ which was started in 2007 by a group of parents with a dream of a different school. Started with 16 pupils, it now has 500 who are each responsible for their own learning. Instead of standing at the front and telling the children what they need to learn, the teachers act as mentors and coaches and only 'teach' when required. Much of the assistance that pupils need comes from their peers, and they are free to decide where to focus the balance of their time. If they are struggling in maths, then they can spend more time on that subject than others. Equally, they can cover the basic concepts or, if they choose, they can study at a more advanced level. Each child has clear expectations of what they should achieve through the year, they set their own goals and attend a tutorial each week. As teachers spend less time teaching classes, the level of tutoring that they can give to each child is far greater than in a traditional school. There are many initiatives within the ESBZ school that make it unique and effective (including giving teachers more autonomy), but it is an example of how, within a bureaucratic system, it is possible to create an environment for the future.

This change of approach is required. At a May 2018 meeting in Madrid, the Managing Director of a Spanish regional trade association pointed out that their partner companies had 200 vacancies that they couldn't fill – despite a youth unemployment rate of 36% in Spain.[xii] The reason was that they couldn't find young people with sufficient basic skills or appropriate attitude to undertake the work required. He rounded on the educationalists in the room and begged them to change the way children are taught to prepare them for work.

This does not mean that we should only focus on teaching children business skills, but rather the skills and attitude to thrive in the future – both inside and outside of the commercial world.

There are many examples of progressive schools, and even countrywide educational systems (eg in Singapore and Finland)[xiii], where the value of education is not only understood but prioritised. However, the ideal that teaching is viewed as one of the most prestigious jobs in the country with pay to match, is unlikely to be enacted in most of the rest of the world anytime soon. As a result, many educational systems may make superficial changes (sufficient to remove a sense of security among teachers), but they retain the core practice of trying to fill a child's head with a pre-set amount and range of knowledge.

Just like the technological, business and social challenges, there is no easy fix to the educational challenges that we face today. To accommodate the changes ahead, we must change our approach to life and work – and for that it is important to understand what it means to be WEIRD.

B) BEING WEIRD

"Don't worry about not fitting in. The things that make people think you're weird are what makes you you, and therefore your greatest strength."
Birgitte Hjort Sorensen – Actress

The challenges outlined in the section above require a different approach to work and therefore a change in our mentality. Although it is not possible for people to change their mindset overnight, there are – and I have implemented within Pod Group – tools to help us take control of our own destiny and start making the changes that will ensure future success.

I am a firm believer in the human spirit and in my view almost anyone, if given the right environment and a little encouragement, can flourish.

Outside one of our offices we have a poem by Christopher Logue (often misattributed to Guillaume Apollinaire):

> Come to the edge.
> We might fall.
> Come to the edge.
> It's too high!
> COME TO THE EDGE!
> And they came
> And he pushed
> And they flew.

After starting the implementation of our own self-management policies at my company, a friend sent me an article, basically hinting that it couldn't work. It was written by a New York business owner who had implemented a policy of working at home on a Friday for his employees. He was then frustrated and angry that employees weren't available at short notice to go to client meetings. The problem wasn't the work at home policy, but rather that it didn't go far enough. Telling people when they should work at home is the same as telling them when they should work in the office – some work is better suited to the office, some to the home – but individuals are better at making that decision than bosses. Expecting people to work at home in the same way as at the office was his second mistake – we all work differently. His third was more fundamental – he clearly couldn't stop controlling his employees, so why was he implementing this policy in the first place?

And this is the point: to overcome the technical, business and social challenges we will face over the next fifteen years, we need to provide an environment where employees feel and behave like business owners – not provide lip service by introducing a policy of working at home on Fridays.

If you are looking for a formula or a prescriptive list of actions to prepare your organisation for the future, you won't find it. The reason is simple: we need to allow employees to decide how they want to work. As we are dealing with people, not computers, we can't use Artificial Intelligence or processes to implement that change.

That said, there are various ways to encourage employees to think and work differently, such as choosing their own salary, but these are the tools, not the goals.

What is required is a way of working that springs from encouraging people to think differently. Within our company, we use WEIRD, which is an acronym for the attitudes we encourage. Specifically:

WISDOM   Encouraging the thought process of 'Is that a wise decision?' encourages an attitude of taking into account all the implications of taking that decision.

 EMOTIONAL INTELLIGENCE   Employees should be encouraged to use their emotional intelligence, display empathy and try to understand other employees. Teamwork can then flow much better.

 **I**NITIATIVE   Initiative is the reverse side of control. A company cannot have control and expect employees to take initiative.

 RESPONSIBILITY   If you expect somebody to take on responsibility, you also need to let that person have the freedom to implement that responsibility in a way they see fit.

 DEVELOPMENT (SELF)   Two thirds of the motivation of an employee comes from the satisfaction of doing a good job, being recognised as such and growing personally as a result.

I have covered each of these characteristics in brief below, so as to keep them in mind whilst exploring the technical, business, social and educational changes that society needs to make.

Wisdom

"The only true wisdom is in knowing you know nothing." I find this quote from Socrates particularly apt when I move to a new country. For the first six months, I feel I don't understand anything.

After six months, I think I know how the country works. After two years I realise that I know very little. At that point, I am beginning to gain enough experience to assess the probability of making a wise decision and to know when to seek advice. Encouraging people to use experience, whilst understanding the limits of their knowledge, should avoid the tendency to do something simply because they have been told to.

Emotional Intelligence

The 'E' in WEIRD could have also meant empathy, but employees (including CEOs) need to exert higher levels of Emotional Intelligence than just empathy. The term Emotional Intelligence (also known as EQ or EI) was popularised by Daniel Goleman in his 1996 book 'Emotional Intelligence'[xiv]. It includes self-awareness, self-regulation, motivation, empathy and social skills.

Organisations are made up of people and, although many companies have prospered by using labour as a commodity, there have always been a few people with high levels of Emotional Intelligence who have been key to creating the spark – whether that is an understanding of what customers want, or the ability to make teams work together. Ignoring Emotional Intelligence was fine for a company in the 19th century but would be disastrous for the future.

As shown in the next chapter, Artificial Intelligence will always struggle with using Emotional Intelligence, not least because computers cannot feel in the same way as people. For example, human beings send strong messages such as 'I'm approachable' or 'stay away'[xv] through very subtle body language. Non-verbal communication includes: facial expressions, gestures, paralinguistics (how you say things), body language, posture, proxemics (personal space), eye gaze, haptics (touch), appearance and artefacts (what objects represent you). In theory a computer could process all of the different non-verbal parameters listed above, but inputting these data in real time would be extremely difficult. Reacting with appropriate non-verbal communication would obviously be hard for a computer to achieve unless it looks like a person. It is also difficult for a robot to interpret non-verbal communications – not least due to the huge number of interpretations available. For example, a white and sweaty face could indicate anxiety – or too much coffee. Lisa Feldman Barrett has a very interesting TED talk about why it is difficult to read emotions.[xvi]

However, human beings are far from perfect. Everybody has different levels of Emotional Intelligence and different reactions to individual circumstances. Add to this the fact that we have our own biases and motivations and it becomes clear why getting teams to work harmoniously together is a complex task.

If employees can be encouraged to use their Emotional Intelligence, display empathy and try to understand why other employees are reacting in a certain way, or realise when colleagues could use help, then teamwork flows much better.

Ricardo Semler[xvii] explains that, if a question can't stand up to three 'whys', it is not required. This is a superb way of removing bureaucracy. However, it can also be used in matters of Emotional Intelligence to identify the wrong question:

Q1: Why is John blocking my work today?
A1: Because John is in a bad mood.
Q2: Why is he directing this at me?
A2: Because we had a disagreement yesterday.
Q3: Why did we have a disagreement?
A3: Because I told him his idea wouldn't be profitable.
OK, So let me ask him how I can help on his idea.

Initiative

Initiative is the reverse side of control. Let people take initiative and you lose control. Keep control and people won't take initiative. A company cannot have control and expect employees to take initiative.

History provides us with numerous examples in which control and a lack of initiative have not ended well. One of the most famous British military disasters was immortalised in Sir Alfred Tennyson's 1854 poem 'The Charge of the Light Brigade'. Captain Louis Nolan carried a message from the commander of British forces, Lord Raglan, to the Light Brigade to ensure that the Russians did not capture Turkish guns from overrun positions. Unfortunately, Nolan did not pass these orders on clearly, and thus the Light Brigade went into 'The Valley of Death' and was fired upon from both sides, suffering huge casualties. To lay blame after the event, Raglan questioned why the commander did not exercise his discretion (or use initiative). Like many leaders, Raglan had never previously given any of his officers the freedom to take initiative and was then surprised when they didn't do so when required.

Many companies try to create an environment where employees can use their initiative within boundaries. This is not initiative, it is providing some flexibility within parameters and certainly will not lead to the type of initiative required to cope with the future.

As an employee, it is especially demoralising to be told to take the initiative and then be criticised for overstepping boundaries which hadn't been established.

It is vital that CEOs, leaders and managers support initiative from employees – even when it was a bad initiative. People learn far more from mistakes than good outcomes, so it is absolutely imperative that, when a bad decision or initiative has been taken, the leader can say:

"It was brilliant that you took the initiative – well done. Unfortunately, it didn't work out but we learnt a lot from that.

Don't let this result stop you from taking initiative again in the future."

The reverse is when somebody has taken the initiative and it has worked out well. I find this one of the most satisfying and motivational compliments that a CEO can give:

"Well done on taking the initiative. It was a great decision and you should be really proud that you did off your own bat. Keep doing it!"

If a leader or manager shows that they are upset when an initiative taken is contrary to company policy, resulted in more work or is a threat to their authority (though they will phrase it differently using any convenient excuse) – then no further initiative will ever be taken by that employee.

Herein lies the problem: it is incredibly easy to stamp out initiative with one remark, but stimulating initiative requires constant encouragement from the top.

A positive outcome from a change created internally or by an unexpected step of initiative has a far greater effect than keeping the status quo. Taking initiative may mean changing something that has been set in stone within the company, and yet is badly thought out, illogical or no longer valid. When an employee takes initiative that creates change then, normally, the outcome is time saved. When that includes time saved for the customer, the customer will appreciate it and become an advocate of the company. Likewise, the individual who took the initiative will feel greater responsibility and ownership towards the company.

Responsibility

Responsibility is a double-edged sword – the other edge is freedom.

Early on in our change towards WEIRD, I listened to a wonderful conversation between two of our developers. First, a little background. Our holiday policy is very simple – we don't have one. Our employees take holidays whenever they like even at short notice; as long as they don't leave their colleagues with more work or unexpected stress.

One of our developers was complaining to the other,

"I don't know what to do about my holidays."

"What's the problem?"

"I take more holiday than you."

"So what?"

"But having the freedom to take holidays when I want is a lot of responsibility."

I was smirking to myself and secretly very pleased that somebody who had come from a very 'command and control' working culture was realising the ups and downs of taking control of their own work life.

There is a direct correlation between responsibility and freedom – the more of one that you have, the more the other comes as part of the package.

To sell the promise of freedom without the necessity for responsibility is selling a false dream. On the other hand, if you expect somebody to take on responsibility, you also need to let that person have the freedom to implement it as they see fit.

When we went through the process of implementing WEIRD, there were two people who said that they did not want responsibility. They said that they preferred to be told what to do so that they could turn up to work and not have to get too involved – ie do what they were asked to do and go home.

We have not restricted their freedom in response to their lack of desire for responsibility. In fact, one of them has been working a lot from home over the last couple of months due to a newborn child.

Despite their concerns, they have proved to be as committed as anybody else in the company. Is that due to the environment, people's innate desire to be in charge of their own destiny or evidence that, if you trust people, then that trust will be returned? I cannot say for sure but, with a few exceptions, I am a firm believer that if you provide people with the freedom to take charge of their own lives – they will understand and accept the responsibility that comes with that.

Development (Self)

Companies, rather like parents, find it hard to resist the desire to mould people to their ideals.

The goal of any for-profit company is, of course, to make money. For me, the most fulfilling (and arguably most effective) way to achieve this is to bring out the best in each employee and let them develop their full potential.

This will not always, however, reflect the role that the company perceives to be the most useful for that individual. For example, the company needs somebody in operations to become a specialist in a specific ticketing system. John would be the best person as he is already dealing with tickets – so John is sent on a training course. The only problem is that John is concerned that becoming a specialist in ticketing is going to narrow his career options.

Within Pod Group, we had an example of keeping somebody in a role they didn't want. Our Greek HR Director (and co-conspirator in WEIRD) joined the company and was allocated the task of invoicing. He is really good at spreadsheets and so, throughout his working life (after doing various training courses on spreadsheets), he was given roles that related to finance. The only problem was that he hated these roles. Ironically, throughout his career, people had said "You're really good with people, now go and do spreadsheets." When we grew sufficiently that we needed a full time HR Director, he pushed himself forward to take on the role and now reads voraciously on the subject. The only problem (for him) is, as he states: "Now that I have the chance to do what I always wanted and said I could do – I have no excuse not to do a good job."

By focusing on his personal development goals before the company goals, we have ended up with a very motivated employee.

An employee engagement firm surveyed 200,000 people across 500 companies.[xviii] One of the questions asked was "What motivates you to excel and go the extra mile at your organization?"

The responses were interesting, if not entirely surprising:

Table 1.1 What motivates employees

Camaraderie, peer motivation	20 %		
Intrinsic desire to a good job	17 %		Satisfaction of doing a good job, being recognised as such and growing personally as a result
Feeling encouraged and recognised	13 %	**68 %**	
Having a real impact	10 %		
Growing professionally	8 %		
Meeting client/customer needs	8 %		
Money and benefits	7 %		
Positive supervisor/senior management	4 %	**32 %**	
Belief in the company/product	4 %		
Other	9 %		

This suggests that over two thirds of the motivation of an employee comes from the satisfaction of doing a good job, being recognised as such and growing personally as a result.

I have always learnt 'on the job' and frequently from things I do badly. Luckily, for most of my career, I have been accountable primarily to myself, so I have had the freedom to make mistakes often. If an employee is allowed to make mistakes, their harshest critic will be themselves – as long as they have been given the authority to be responsible for themselves in the first place.

I can guarantee that when employees know they are 100% responsible for the decisions they make, they will make better decisions. Why? Because they will go back to the beginning of the WEIRD process and ask themselves: *Is this wise?*

Circling through WEIRD

To recap on the WEIRD attitude:

Any decision-making process first starts with an idea. Some of us then act without thinking, but assuming you can avoid that temptation, the first question to ask is:

Is this wise?

Thereafter, as you think through the implications, you need to use your Emotional Intelligence to consider the human aspects of your decision. Especially:

How is this decision going to affect others? Who is going to be affected? What can I do to smooth the path before implementing this decision? (The answer to this is easy – seek advice.)

Once you have sought advice and feel more confident, then you need to take the initiative and implement the decision.

Making a decision is usually the first part of the journey; therefore, you need to own the decision and its implementation. It is important to be responsible for, rather than defensive about, your decision.

Finally, each decision you take feeds into your own self-development, so you need to review each decision and its implementation so that you can be a little wiser for next time. How to circle through the WEIRD attributes is shown below.

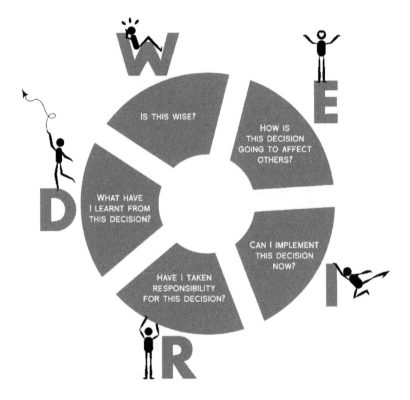

To quote John F. Kennedy: "*For time and the world do not stand still. Change is the law of life.*" This is particularly true today and will be even more so in the coming years. It is therefore worth exploring in more detail why we need to implement WEIRD practices. The first reason is due to the technological changes that we will experience within the future of work.

Chapter 2

TECHNOLOGICAL CHANGE

"Technology is a useful servant but a dangerous master."
Christian Lous Lange – Norwegian historian

A) FROM THE FIRST TO THE FOURTH INDUSTRIAL REVOLUTION

"Every industrial revolution brings along a learning revolution."
Alexander De Croo – Flemish politician

We are currently in the middle of the fourth industrial revolution.

The first started at the end of the 18th century with the invention of steam driven engines that led to mechanisation. William Blake refers to the cotton and other factories that were created as a result of this mechanisation in the Midlands and North of England as "those dark satanic mills".[i]

Not a great accolade to advancement. As agriculture became more mechanised and the number of jobs in the fields plummeted, workers sought employment in factories. However, it took a generation for employment to reach an acceptable level as people adjusted to the new way of working.

The creation of the motor car by Henry Ford at the beginning of the 20th century was a consequence of the second industrial revolution which evolved out of electrically powered mass production.[i] However, Ford grasped more than the power of electricity; he understood the power of marketing and, specifically, the importance of creating a product to signify status. He also recognised the importance of creating a consumer (or middle) class; and to help generate this class, he deliberately paid his workers sufficiently such that, in time, they could own their own Ford motor car.[ii]

As depicted in the 2016 film *Hidden Figures*, the mathematicians who spent their working hours calculating complicated equations within NASA in the 1960s were known as 'computers'. The end of the film marks the start of the third industrial revolution with the installation of an IBM computer at NASA to replace the human 'computers'.

Until the financial crisis of 2008, the automation of many tasks by computers was mostly about making incremental productivity improvements. Some jobs were lost but, with employment at a reasonably high level in Western countries, those displaced were able to find alternative employment and the productivity gains heralded more economic activity. A virtuous circle was created that economists strive to achieve, and for which politicians take credit.

We are still in the midst of those productivity improvements, but we are also beginning to witness the fourth industrial revolution, which will fundamentally change the way we interact with computers.[iii]

Until recently, actions undertaken by a computer had to be instigated by a human being. Now, however, computers are undertaking tasks autonomously. For many tasks, computers act as a dumb (albeit very quick) data processing aide but they are starting to be used such that the physical, digital and biological worlds can interact in ways that we are only beginning to conceive. As Klaus Schwab mentions in the description of his 2016 book *The Fourth Industrial Revolution*, "we are even challenging ideas about what it means to be human".[iv] Prosthetic arms controlled by thoughts alone; nano-technology used to replace worn human parts – technology is affecting the way we work and live in ways that I couldn't have imagined when I started my company 20 years ago.

B) DISRUPTIVE TECHNOLOGIES

"Without question, intelligent technologies will continue to disrupt the world as we know it. There will be profound implications, both positive and negative."
Pierre Nanterme – CEO Accenture

Since I have been running Pod Group, I have seen how technologies can disrupt whole industries and how people's lives are re-shaped as a result. Pod was originally a provider in the mobile data communications industry (although we have now extended beyond this) which provides the backbone for many of the disruptive technologies that have appeared over the last few years. Our customers build solutions for the Internet of Things (IoT). However, before IoT, there was Machine-to-Machine (M2M) and prior to that, Telematics (as most applications were related to vehicles). Whilst each of these terms refers to different parts of remote monitoring, they have mostly superseded each other. By taking the example of monitoring vehicles, it is possible to gain not only a good picture of how technology has evolved, but also a glimpse of how industries (and workers) that depend upon vehicles will fare.

GPS devices have been available for many years, but it was during the late 1990s and in the new millennium that the technology became cheap enough and sensitive enough to be used widely in businesses. GPS trackers were added to high value vehicles and other machinery (such as diggers) in case of theft. However, an intelligent thief found it reasonably easy to follow the wiring and cut power to the device.

Since those early days, three different technological shifts have taken place that have changed the way electronics – including GPS devices – are used. Firstly, GPS chips (similar to other electronics), as well as being cheaper, have become more powerful which allows the device to detect a location inside and independent of weather conditions. Secondly, mobile networks, on which the location of the device is sent back to base, have become more widespread. Thirdly, battery technology has improved hugely,[v] allowing manufacturers to add batteries that replace or complement fixed wiring. The progress of battery technology has allowed the creating of devices that can sit in the field for years without charging or human interaction and communicate occasionally using low powered radio networks.

Due to better and cheaper technology, human imagination and initiative have been set free to create new markets by pulling together different technologies and methodologies.

Let's go back to the example of the GPS tracker. By combining the GPS with scheduling software (which has also improved hugely over the last twenty years due to greater computer processing power), Amazon is able to offer one-hour delivery slots in London compared to 'sometime between nine and five' in the past.

However, disruptive business models don't come about just as a result of combining technologies – they normally require a change in the environment. One reason that Amazon can employ so many delivery people, and Uber has been so successful, is the improvements in scheduling mentioned above combined with something out of their control – namely the reduction in the manufacturing cost of GPS units. This has enabled any smartphone to provide an accurate location – including each Amazon delivery person or Uber driver.

During a recent visit to San Francisco, our Uber driver was a student who did not own a car. By using a car-sharing app, she rented a car by the hour and signed on to Uber and Lyft to offer rides. Working about five hours a day, she earns $100–$200 per shift. Having created employment for herself (albeit with help from Uber), with no capital investment and limited operational investment ($30 in advance to rent the car), she had an income of $2,000 - $4,000 per month working when she wanted to.

In the United States, there are approximately 3.5 million truck drivers (but 8.5 million employed in the industry),[vi] 1.3 million delivery drivers, 250,000 taxi drivers and 715,000 Uber and Lyft drivers.[vii] I haven't included hospital drivers, private taxis etc. Therefore, a conservative estimate of the number of professional drivers in the US would be 6 million. This equates to approximately 5% of the 126 million working population[viii] and doesn't include indirect jobs related to the transportation industry. The UK has a similar percentage of drivers.

These jobs will be lost to self-driving vehicles - I will explain why.[ix]

First the technology. Self-driving cars use hundreds of sensors to record everything going on around the car. These are combined with radar and cameras which transmit all this information to computers within the car. Then the clever stuff starts – the information is used both as a learning tool and a driving tool. Google has a fleet of vehicles that have collectively driven millions of miles gathering information about all the different scenarios that *could* happen on the road. For example, who could have predicted scenes such as a person in a wheelchair chasing a duck across the road… and then chasing it back again… and then chasing it in circles. If you are wondering what the car did – well it did nothing until the duck had been chased off the road.[x]

Tesla has taken a different route. On its newer vehicles, Tesla runs its autopilot software in the background, which simulates the car driving autonomously in real time and compares what could have happened to what did happen. This information is sent to Tesla for each car manufactured after October 2016 (some earlier Tesla cars also send information). I would estimate that Tesla has over 2 billion miles (billion not million) of shadow data. After receiving the data, Tesla uses Machine Learning to improve its autonomous driving software; and then updates cars already in the field to test and further improve the new code.

It would take the average driver about 166 million years to gain the same driving experience as that of a Tesla car.

The number of accidents caused by Google Cars (now called Waymo) is practically zero. Almost all the accidents in which Waymo cars have been involved were caused by other drivers; likewise for Tesla.[xi] Sadly, in March 2018, the first pedestrian fatality happened involving an Uber self-driving vehicle in autonomous mode which hit a pedestrian in Arizona. Unfortunately, the accompanying human driver also failed to react. Accusations have arisen that autonomous cars are unsafe – and they need further improvement. However, the low number of accidents caused by autonomous vehicles compares to an average over the last couple of years of one accident per 150,000 miles driven by people – resulting in 2.35 million crash-related injuries per year in the United States and 200,000 in the United Kingdom.

The law is finally catching up. By the time this book is published, self-driving cars will be permitted on roads within the United States, Estonia and other countries with some conditions. So as Elon Musk, the founder of Tesla, has questioned, "When will human driven cars be banned from the road as unsafe?"[xii] In time, driving will become a hobby in the same way as horse riding changed from a means of transport to a sport. I am not sure how motor racing enthusiasts will feel about a human racing driver being beaten by a self-driving car, but in the same way that IBM's chess playing Deep Blue beat Garry Kasparov, the fastest driver in the world will soon be a computer.

People at IBM have continued to try and disrupt the technology of the present. One tool that they are using to achieve this is the IBM Watson Artificial Intelligence platform[xiii]. I always assumed that this was named after the Watson of Sherlock Holmes fame, but apparently it was named after IBM's first CEO – Thomas J. Watson. IBM Watson is trying to replicate the human brain and combine it with huge processing power to allow developers to create applications that currently exist only in futurist films.

As human beings we can either accept that technology is going to disrupt our lives, or we can bury our heads in the sand. However, it is not a computer that decides to be the fastest driver – but rather a person (or a team of people) that has the vision, embraces the future and will persist until they have achieved their goal. Generation Z and younger millennials are natively comfortable with technology, embrace disruptive technologies and will ensure that change happens. The opportunity for employers lies in understanding this, giving employees the freedom to make decisions and recognising them for the changes they make.

It can be difficult for those from Generation X to appreciate that the speed of technology is increasing exponentially and company strategies need to change ever more rapidly. The last strategy I set out in our annual meeting lasted four months before we realised it didn't fit the market any more. Part of the reason for this speed of change lies in the rate at which processing power is growing and opening up new opportunities. This is covered in the next chapter.

C) *COMPUTERS, BIG DATA & IOT*

"Computers are like Old Testament gods: lots of rules and no mercy."
Joseph Campbell – Author

Computers cannot surpass the human brain in all aspects – which is the reason for this book. Regardless, many computer scientists are trying to simulate human thought processes in computer models using Cognitive Computing.[xiv] I will return to the related practicalities and limitations later but, for now, it is worth looking at the developments and possibilities around cognitive computing, Artificial Intelligence and raw data processing power.

In 1965, the co-founder of Intel stated that the number of transistors on a circuit board would double approximately every two years (this became known as Moore's law). He was wrong in only one aspect – it was closer to eighteen months. To paraphrase this – every 18 months computers have double the processing power.

It is this huge increase in processing power that allows us to run Artificial Intelligence software as well as more bloated software programs. Since 1985 when Windows 1.0 appeared, processing power has increased by between 10,000 and 100,000 times (depending on the chip).[xv] Unfortunately, the latest version of Windows requires 8,000 times more power than Windows 1.0 did – which is why our computers aren't exponentially quicker than in 1985.[xvi]

A couple of years ago, I listened to a talk about an experiment aimed at creating a robot which could build a daughter robot to move 30 centimetres in the shortest time. The mother robot had various sizes of blocks, hinges and batteries available to stick together in order to find the fastest robot offspring. On each attempt, the mother would time the daughter's progress before creating another daughter.

As the experiment unfolded, it became clear that, rather than analysing the performance and making well thought out improvements, this was more of an exercise in trial and error. As the creation of each daughter was automated, the mother was able to create and test hundreds of different versions which had been stuck together in slightly different ways. It wasn't so much an example of Artificial Intelligence as a demonstration of utilising raw processing power.

The most efficient processing machine available today (when you take into account the energy required) is, and will be for some time, the human brain. So how can the efficiency of the human brain be combined with computer processing power so that the brain can be utilised for higher value tasks? Computers can organise, compute and run complicated software – but they are still following instructions rather than thinking. Elon Musk is trying to level the playing field of what he sees as the danger of computers (and specifically Artificial Intelligence) by starting a company called Neuralink[xvii] that is researching the possibilities of brain-machine interfaces (think controlling prosthetic limbs to start with – and controlling everything by thoughts alone after) by adding Artificial Intelligence to human brains.

However, Neuralink's promise of an integrated Human–AI future is some way off, so it is worth looking at how the brain and the computer complement each other today. There are a number of differences as explained in an article at ScienceBlogs:[xviii]

- Brains have an inbuilt retrieval system that can retrieve a full memory with a few cues. Computers by comparison need masses of storage and retrieval capability.
- Brains are not restricted to a limited short-term memory (or RAM)
- Neurons in brains are electrochemical – the chemical part of the signal adds a level of power that computers do not have with electrical signals alone.

- Processing and memory are performed together in the brain but separated in a computer.
- The brain is a self-organising system.
- Brains have bodies which provide senses and other advantages.
- Brains are bigger than any current standard computer.

This simplified list of differences indicates why human brains are considerably more advanced than computers. Although computers will become more powerful, human brains will continue to have the ability to retrieve, sense and organise in a manner that, in computers, will be restricted by the amount of data and processing power available. It is these human capabilities that need to be encouraged in the workplace, while maximising the use of computers to undertake routine tasks that don't require human intervention. However, the use of these capabilities relies on people being given the freedom to make their own decisions – and to retrieve, sense and organise their thoughts in the way they see fit for the benefit of each individual task or project. Using these capabilities will allow us to make best use of what computers can do.

So, what can a computer do?

First and foremost, computers are very good at following instructions. So long as the data are inserted into the computer in a format it can understand then it will be able to process the data as fast as its processor will allow. Sooner or later it will regurgitate the information you require. However, if the information that the computer is trying to process isn't exactly as it expects, then you can experience the frustration that leads to wanting to throw the damn machine out of the window (remembering to open the window first!).

Currently, when an application doesn't perform as expected, a person needs to look at the code and make a fix. In the future, however, this role will be replaced by a program designed for that purpose.

Companies providing Cloud computing servers (with huge warehouses of computers) would until recently have, for example, 200 engineers maintaining these servers. Now that is likely to be nearer to five engineers. Computer engineers have written programs that constantly monitor all servers, identify broken bits of code, decide on the best fix and automatically apply the appropriate patch.

Although this monitoring application has replaced around 195 engineers, it is not making any decisions on its own. The actions that it can take are dependent upon the decisions of the person who wrote the application. The reason for the continued employment of the remaining five people is to replace physical parts and to add or fix code if an unexpected bug arises. As more and more fixes are coded, the team may reduce to, say, three people. Which brings up an interesting motivational quandary when you know you are coding yourself out of a job?

So, what else can a computer do? Actually, not a lot. A computer will only do what it has been programmed to do.

However, adding Artificial Intelligence and more specifically Machine Learning changes a computer from being dumb to smart(er) – this is covered in the next chapter. A standard application's purpose is to provide pre-set responses to pre-set commands. A Machine Learning application will allow for questions (commands) that may not fit the pre-set responses and try to calculate the best answer. Although it may be very frustrating to go through twelve suggestions (none of which work) before you can ask a person why your computer won't play Netflix on your TV, you have provided valuable information to a Machine Learning application – namely that none of the suggestions worked. If you had solved your problem on the third suggestion and many other people experienced the same issue at the same time, then the application will have learnt that a significant number of people are suffering a known issue and an update needs to be sent to all computers running that particular version of the software.

But for an application to learn, it needs data; indeed without huge amounts of data, Machine Learning and especially Deep Learning could not have reached its current stage of development.

Which is why we collect what has become known as 'Big Data'. So, what is Big Data and why does it matter?

Big Data is as described – huge amounts of data so voluminous that they cannot be handled using standard processing methods. An often-quoted statistic (that I suspect is underestimating the reality) is that 90% of the data in the world has been produced in the last two years[xix]. Fifteen years ago, the largest datasets were input into very structured databases (including spreadsheets). Today, however, data arrives from all aspects of our lives – where we are (through the map on our phone), where we shop and what we buy, what we watch, what we search for online, our medical conditions, who we talk to and what we say online – the list goes on.

Whilst the image of a joined up dystopian world where the authorities (or big tech companies) know everything we are doing at all times is often portrayed in the press, the reality is rather different. Each company has information related to what they are doing – so, for example, Amazon knows about each consumer for shopping habits, Netflix for viewing, Google for online searching and Facebook for social media.

But within each of these specialist areas, the data are incredibly valuable – mainly because they can be compared to other data from the whole user base. Big Data has become so important in today's world (often described as the new gold) that the cost of holding data is now low compared to the potential value.

The ability to gather huge quantities of data opens up the opportunity to run models that can compare millions of pieces of information. By creating simulations and changing inputs, it is possible to see how results differ. It is this combination of data and processing power that increases the possibility of finding a pattern or insight, predicting behaviour, making assumptions backed up by hard evidence and recognising patterns.

But the true value of Big Data is in understanding how to mine it. Experienced data mining analysts can easily earn a six- or even seven-figure salary, which gives an indication as to the value of the analysis that can be generated from the data.

By joining data from multiple sources, the value grows exponentially. For example, a company such as Unilever will combine data from social media and focus groups with that from test markets to understand the potential success of new products.

Big Data is equally relevant to industry. Data from factories are collated to understand when machines need maintenance or are likely to break down, often being updated remotely and avoiding vast expense in relation to factory shut downs and engineer call outs.

The ability to send updates and do other things automatically is the basis of the Internet of Things (IoT) – lots of devices working autonomously. IoT devices also provide much of the Big Data mentioned above.

One of the divisions within our company provides mobile connectivity for the IoT. This allows information on devices on the move or dispersed across the world to be transmitted to a central computer (previously an engineer would have gone out to physically collect the data). The data are then analysed by programs and the information is diced and turned to provide locations, temperatures, alarms, predictive movement, passenger information, credit card information, advertising placement, refill schedules, time to harvest, state of bee hives – the list goes on.

IoT is a ridiculously overused acronym that seems to capture anything futuristic. In reality it relates to a lot of sensors connected to processors that transmit the data to a central server. Some of the data may then be joined with other data to become Big Data.

The reasons for collecting the data vary enormously. For example, it may be necessary to monitor the location of a delivery truck to adjust delivery schedules in real time and inform customers of amended drop off times.

Sensors are used in vending machines and bars so that there is no need for daily checks to restock the machine. These and the much-quoted restocking fridge (I've yet to meet anybody who owns one) are examples of the most basic uses of IoT.

One of the more interesting applications that we support is the monitoring of bees. By using sensors it is possible to monitor the amount of honey produced, temperature and humidity, whether the queen is still laying and other information about the hive. Add in some intelligence and other related (Big) data, and much more can be predicted such as colony strength, foraging activity, forage shortages, effect of weather conditions – all compared to other hives around the world. Albert Einstein famously predicted that "if the bees disappeared off the face of the earth, man would only have four years left to live." Whilst many would disagree with this assertion, the health of bees is a good predictor of the health of the world.

One of our other clients monitors ski resorts for avalanches. By monitoring snowfall and weather conditions using sensors in the mountain, the company can predict when an avalanche is likely to occur, allowing the authorities to create a controlled avalanche when nobody is on the mountain.

So how is IoT, especially combined with Big Data, Artificial Intelligence, Machine Learning and Deep Learning going to change the future of work and obliterate a large number of jobs?

As always, the main driver is economics. The cost of basic devices which undertake limited processing activities and forward the data via mobile networks is becoming minimal. Likewise, connected sensors for basic monitoring are very low cost when purchased in big volumes.[xx] Low powered networks are bringing down the operational costs of IoT by sending small amounts of data from units running for up to 20 years on standard batteries without any human interaction. Low powered radio devices have already become so cheap that building companies are looking to embed sensors into the concrete of new buildings to monitor for future structural weaknesses.[xxi]

So, is the IoT a threat to jobs? In short, yes.

Using technology remotely to monitor vending machines, collect meter readings, ensure successful deliveries and countless other examples has already created huge efficiencies, reducing the number of people who would have previously undertaken these tasks.

To date these job losses have been absorbed by further growth in the economy (an economist's dream). Increased efficiency has allowed investment into new goods and services which in turn has created new jobs[xxii]. However, the present efficiencies will be minor compared to what will be achieved when IoT, Big Data and Artificial Intelligence are optimised together. IoT will allow sensors around the world to provide huge amounts of information to form Big Data; and Artificial Intelligence will then be used to process and manipulate the data and create efficiencies in every aspect of our lives.

These efficiencies will result in a level of job losses that will be difficult to replace. We have a little breathing space to change the way that we work, because much of what we think of today as Artificial Intelligence isn't so much intelligence as processing power. However Machine Learning, a subset of Artificial Intelligence that combines processing power with a level of intelligence, will minimise the need for human intervention still further. To understand why we need to change our way of working to optimise the use of Machine and Deep Learning, we first need to understand how they function.

D) MACHINE LEARNING AND DEEP LEARNING

"People worry that computers will get too smart and take over the world, but the real problem is that they're too stupid and they've already taken over the world."
Pedro Domingos – Professor, Machine Learning

Machine Learning uses the key advantages that computers hold over people – speed, accuracy and a lack of bias – whilst adding in some human classification skills. Human beings store thoughts, memories and ideas in different parts of the brain. This ability to categorise information allows for easy recall and the ability to predict and weigh the probability of future outcomes. It is this that Machine Learning (and Deep Learning as a subset of Machine Learning) is trying to emulate.

Machine Learning is a key part of both Google's Gmail spam filtering and Amazon's shopping recommendations. Gmail's spam filtering claims a 99.9% success rate in blocking unwanted emails.[xxiii] But what is spam? One person's spam is the next person's new purchase (although the opportunity to collect $100 million from a deposed African dictator is generally spam to everybody), which is why individualised Machine Learning has value. It works by providing a computer with a base of data in which the (in this case) spam is already identified. More emails are then fed into the computer which identifies what it thinks is spam. The third step is to correct the computer's predictions so that it can re-categorise the email and learn for next time. Obviously, the more data that the computer can learn from, the faster the Machine Learning process is – which puts Google with its 1.2 billion Gmail users at a considerable advantage. However, what is so powerful about Gmail is not that it blocks spam and identifies promotional messages so effectively, but rather that it does so on an individualised basis. Each time we identify an email as not being spam or something that we want to buy – it is learning our personal preferences.

At times this Machine Learning capability may seem too intrusive in our lives, inciting a desire to escape to a remote island without electricity or internet and read a book by candle light. However, it can be used to very good effect – especially in medicine. Some cancers, for example, are difficult to treat because they are diagnosed too late. The use of Artificial Intelligence within search engines is providing some interesting possibilities. Researchers from Microsoft looked at the search terms used by those who had made a search on pancreatic cancer. They estimated that, in 5–15% of cases, they could predict pancreatic cancer substantially prior to the official diagnosis and before the search term 'pancreatic cancer' was used. People with a propensity to suffer pancreatic cancer are also likely to have stomach pains and itchiness – these search terms combined with the timing of the searches provided the clues. With Microsoft's predicted false positive rate of 1 in 100,000 and the possibility of knowing a crucial number of weeks earlier – which could be the difference between life and death – wouldn't you want to know?[xxiv]

Furthermore, no doctor has time to keep abreast of all the latest research and information in their field. This compares to IBM Watson that has learnt, amongst other things, the 23 million medical papers stored in Medline and can retrieve any one of them in milliseconds.[xxv] This is partly why a computer is accurate 90% of the time in assessing lung cancer compared to 50% by a human doctor.

We are still at the early stages of knowing what the future holds for Artificial Intelligence within medicine but, given that misdiagnosis is the third leading cause of death after heart disease and cancer in the United States,[xxvi] computer diagnostics will (and should) become more relied upon.

This success in saving lives and increasing longevity does obviously create a side effect – overpopulation. Optimists assure us that this can be resolved by making the world a more efficient place and this is where sensors around the world (IoT) creating data (Big Data) which can be analysed (Artificial Intelligence) contribute. They will identify where waste can be cut, and productivity raised.

The next chapter covers examples of where Machine Learning and Artificial Intelligence will take over some of the roles in today's office by incorporating pre-determined decisions. However, Machine Learning requires human initiative to understand and plan the results. It is this initiative, combined with other WEIRD attributes such as Emotional Intelligence, that will be required of employees to complement the output from Machine Learning algorithms.

Even greater opportunities arise if we look at the possibilities of Deep Learning, a branch of Machine Learning that will lead to developments that scare the innocent (and sometimes those in the know as well).

To date there are still limited applications making use of Deep Learning. However, more affordable processing power and advances in Deep Learning techniques will ensure that it becomes more mainstream.

So how does Deep Learning differ from Machine Learning? Think back to how Tesla and Google developed the software for running their self-driving cars – it was primarily written by engineers. In 2016, the chipmaker Nvidia tested a self-driving car in Monmouth County, New Jersey.[xxvii] The difference between this and the Tesla or Google cars is that it used an algorithm and taught itself how to drive by watching people.

Mount Sinai Hospital in New York took the hospital's database of 700,000 patient records to train a Deep Learning program called Deep Patient.[xxviii] The researchers did not write a program to analyse pre-determined queries but rather wrote an algorithm and left the Deep Learning program to find patterns. It proved to be far more effective at predicting when people were likely to get a disease, including cancer of the liver, than a doctor. It also was better at predicting schizophrenia. The problem with Deep Learning is that because, like us, it teaches itself, it sometimes makes predictions and decisions that cannot be explained. The instigators of Deep Patient don't know, for example, why it is good at predicting psychiatric conditions.

We need to understand how to cope in the world of the future and Deep Learning will have a role in this; it will destroy jobs and have profound changes on work and society as we know them. Therefore we should take it into account when we consider how and what we need to change.

So how does Deep Learning work?

The inspiration for Deep Learning comes from the human brain[xxix] which hosts approximately 100 billion neurons. These communicate with other neurons via synaptic connections.

Neural networks in computers work the same way, but instead of sending an electrochemical signal they send a weighted number to signify the level of confidence. The weighted number relates to the route by which the signals have been sent, but basically it comes down to a level of certainty. Let us imagine that you live in a nature reserve and want to create a retractable fence that will only spring out of the ground if an animal comes within five meters. To create a Deep Learning algorithm to recognise people and keep out animals, you load lots of images of people (labelled 'human') and animals and other images (labelled 'not human').

Each image would be broken down into its composite parts and analysed (colour, lines, angles etc.) through an input layer. These are then passed on to hidden layers which recognise or do not recognise each attribute. This recognition or non-recognition is multiplied by the weight (certainty) of that hidden layer recognising that attribute. Finally, the information is passed to an output layer which can indicate, with a level of confidence, whether or not it is a human being.

On the principle that a picture speaks a thousand words, I hope the graphic below will complement the words above.

Table 2.1: Understanding Deep Learning

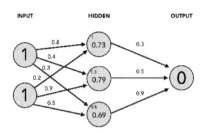

Source: Cosmos Magazine

In people, the older we get the harder it is to change the synaptic connections in the brain because they get stronger the more they are used. A neural network algorithm has a far more efficient feedback mechanism that allows it to change the weighting of a synaptic connection quickly if the final output (eg gorilla, not human) is wrong. As computers aren't proud and don't mind being proved wrong, it is easier to re-program the synaptic connection of a computer than of a person.

Supervised Deep Learning needs some element of human interaction because the algorithm has to be told whether the answer is correct or not.[xxx]

The alternative is Unsupervised Deep Learning. In the example above, by providing initial examples of what is and is not a human being, the Deep Learning algorithm is supervised. With Unsupervised Deep Learning you provide the input and leave the computer on its own to see what patterns the algorithm produces. In the example above, it would probably be able to categorise people, but it might also identify mammals that can stand on two legs, or that people who look older are slightly more bent over than younger people, or that those who look pale are about to fall ill (especially if an additional input of illnesses was added) – in fact it may come up with a range of interesting patterns that we would never have thought of.[xxxi]

Thankfully, unless a trigger is linked to the output of an Unsupervised Deep Learning algorithm, we still need to do something with the analysis.

One of the worrying aspects of Deep Learning is that it is not clear how the algorithm is conducting the steps between the input provided and the final output.

Therefore, wherever Deep Learning becomes prevalent, issues over responsibility and blame will arise because the decision-making process of the algorithms is not transparent. In fact, even the authors of these programs cannot always explain how the algorithm works. But then again, neither do we know how decisions are reached in the human brain.

However, until these steps do become more transparent, we are not able to understand when there are missing data that may result in a flawed decision. When decisions made by algorithms are wrong, we won't know why or be able to take steps to resolve them. This could lead to serious consequences – think military drones or medical decisions being made based on a faulty algorithm.

The US Defence Advanced Research Projects Agency (DARPA) is currently funding 13 projects specifically around trying to find ways to understand Deep Learning algorithms. One of these, run by Professor Carlos Guestrin at the University of Washington, has instigated a method whereby an algorithm will output examples that reflect its decision-making process.[xxxii] For example, when scanning emails, a few keywords could be highlighted that had a large influence on the decision-making process. The problem with this approach is that it provides simplified explanations for a complex decision-making process. In September 2018, IBM announced a service that would be able to explain how a Deep Learning algorithm reached its decision and what biases had been created within the decision.[xxxiii]

This is particularly important when it comes to assessing the quality of the data used. In 2016, Microsoft launched an Artificial

Intelligence 'teenage girl' bot. Once released onto a cynical world, it was hounded with racist speech, which it interpreted as normal and thus started spewing propaganda.[xxxiv]

Data bias can have a damaging impact beyond teenage girl bots. In the US, a confidential algorithm called COMPAS is used to predict the likelihood of re-offending by criminals[xxxv] as well as to guide the sentencing process. According to analysis undertaken by Pulitzer Prize-winning non-profit news organisation ProPublica, the algorithm had an inaccurate bias as black people re-offend less than the algorithm's prediction and white people re-offend more.

The problem is that the data used to build these algorithms and provide assumptions have a human bias.

It is possible that an algorithm could be programmed to try to overcome this human bias, although this could lead to even greater confusion when trying to understand how the algorithm arrived at a decision. However, if developers do not take account of human bias in the data sets, it will become more and more difficult to fight discrimination as Deep Learning algorithms build upon themselves with flawed data.

Whilst Deep Learning is potentially scary while being full of promise – let's take a reality check. Only 1% of Artificial Intelligence is Machine Learning and only 1% of Machine Learning is Deep Learning.[xxxvi]

E) THE EFFECT OF AUTOMATION

"Automation is good, so long as you know exactly where to put the machine."
Eliyahu Goldratt – Author

The good news is that any mass loss of jobs won't happen overnight. What some may consider to be bad news is that it has already started.[xxxvii]

We are already about 5,000 years into the process, but automation has accelerated significantly in the last 50 years, and even more in the last 5 years. As we start to automate, further automation becomes easier and hence the speed is increasing at an exponential rate.

One of the key indicators of this is the speed of payback for robots. In China this had already dropped from five to three years between 2013 and 2017.[xxxviii] As prices continue to drop, owners are more likely to rely on a computer, that comes with a guarantee and can be easily replaced, than a person that needs training, could leave or fall ill.

So, what will drive this ever-faster uptake of automation?

Firstly, the speed of innovation. Futurist Ray Kurzweil created a formula to work out the total calculations per second (cps) that a human brain can undertake so that this could be compared to a computer.[xxxix] He calculated it at 10 quadrillion cps (in case you are wondering, that is 10 followed by 15 zeros – so quite quick). There is one computer that beats a human brain – built in China with a speed of 34 quadrillion cps at a cost of $390 million and using 24 megawatts of power (the output of a small power station compared to the human brain that needs the same power as a faint light bulb). The cps of a $1,000 computer is about one thousandth that of a human brain but it is worth remembering that, in 2005, the same computer had a millionth; in 1995 a billionth; and in 1985 a trillionth of the speed of the human brain. When will the cps of a $1000 computer surpass a human brain? Probably somewhere around 2025.[xl]

Secondly, more and more investment is being directed towards Artificial Intelligence and robotics. IDC forecasts that worldwide spending on AI hardware, software and services will jump from $12 billion in 2017 to $58 billion by 2021.[xli] Just as venture capitalists in 2000 wanted to invest in a dot com, many now expect an element of Artificial Intelligence in any investment opportunity.

Thirdly is legislation. As mentioned previously, governments have created little legislation around Artificial Intelligence but, when they do, automation will accelerate. It can feel to those outside Silicon Valley or Silicon Fen that corporates are driving innovation policy as governments are slow in embracing new technology.[xlii]

An exception is Estonia, where some innovators prefer to work for the government than for private companies. Estonia has implemented a digital society where almost everything can be done online. Not only does this apply to any interaction with government institutions, but private companies can also interact with user information.

The Estonian government did not try to layer an online environment on top of an existing bureaucratic process, but rather built a digital environment that could be layered upon. One of the key attributes of the system is that no data have to be entered twice, so there is coordination (called X-Road) between multiple databases holding the same information. This makes it easier to provide privacy controls to each user (and citizen) who can see all the information held about them and which organisations have been given permission to access each piece of information. Furthermore, whenever data are requested or viewed by a third party, that enquiry is logged with a record of the viewer. Alerts are created if information is requested that is not deemed necessary to the viewer, and a phone call may be made to ask why the information was accessed.[xliii]

The UK has been trying for years to digitalise medical records within the National Health System[xliv] but is nowhere near the level achieved in Estonia, where not only is information shared within hospitals and available to emergency services, but is automated sufficiently that prescriptions are available at private pharmacists by presenting an ID card and all appropriate discounts are calculated automatically.

Deaths by accident have dropped by 50% in Estonia over the last 20 years[xlv] due to the speed of response by emergency services and to preventive measures. Emergency services can identify the location of an accident victim to within five meters and 93% of calls are answered within ten seconds.

Obviously, this level of digitalisation has led to a loss of jobs but Estonia has made a huge effort to retrain – and now has one of the highest rates of technology employment in Europe. Within such an environment of innovation, high technology employment isn't perhaps a huge surprise – after all Skype was created in Estonia.

Estonia has one major threat. Sharing its eastern border, Russia is keen to extend its influence over the country. As part of NATO, Estonia is a strategically important geopolitical country, and the threat of invasion from Russia is real. It is for this reason (as well as cost) that the Estonian government holds its citizen's information in the Cloud (hosted in a second site in Luxembourg) so that the government could operate virtually if required. Furthermore, by digitalising its citizens' records, Estonia is reckoned to save about 2% of GDP per year, which corresponds to the amount that it spends on defence – mostly to guard against Russia.[xlvi]

This digitalisation has also changed how Estonian society interacts with itself. A level of trust has been introduced both towards the government and towards private enterprise. Because citizens feel that they own their data, an open and more transparent society has been created.

There is no reason (apart from will and politics) why larger countries cannot follow the Estonian model.

Estonia is also one of the first countries to legalise self-driving cars (to date, Level 3 – a human being needs to be in the car).[xlvii] Other countries (including the US and the UK) are moving forward with trials and legislation[xlviii] so it is now a question of when, not if, they become legal. Within five to fifteen years, there will be more self-driving than manually driven cars[xlix] and the number of conventional vehicles will disappear very quickly as they become uneconomical. Therefore, in the decade following self-driving legislation, almost all jobs that require driving skills will be lost.

A study by the World Bank predicted that, globally, 57% of jobs will be lost to automation within the next 20 years.[l] This will affect developing countries with repetitive, low paid jobs to a greater degree than developed countries.

However, as mentioned earlier, within developed countries some jobs will be affected by automation to a greater degree than others. In 2013, Carl Frey and Michael Osborne wrote a paper on those professions most likely to be automated. They may have underestimated the speed of automation in certain industries but their point is valid. Of the 702 professions, 25% have a 90% or above chance of being automated[li] In terms of timeframe, again five to fifteen years would be a good estimate.

There are plenty of studies about job losses in the future. However, there is a better example in the present. By 2018, Amazon had about 100,000 robots. For each robot employed, approximately two jobs are destroyed within companies that compete with Amazon.

The natural assumption is that low skilled jobs will be lost first. However, David Autor from MIT came to a different conclusion.[lii] He pointed out that US employment statistics could be read to suggest that both middle and highly skilled jobs are being steadily replaced by machines. As a higher number of low skilled jobs are being created in the workplace, it creates an illusion of keeping employment numbers high.

The three previous industrial revolutions each caused a loss of manual jobs. There is a good possibility that the fourth one will destroy more office-based than manual jobs. The reason for this can be explained by looking again at IBM Watson, which is trying to replicate human cognitive behaviour. It may eventually match a human brain (although that is debatable) but it will always be limited by a lack of physical attributes – which is why manual jobs may last longer than office jobs.

The potential for automation therefore is not the skill level, but rather the replicability of the job. The more replicable it is – the more likely it is to be lost.

Conversely, the types of jobs that are difficult to replicate are those that require:

    1) Creativity (Scientist, Business Strategist)
    2) Human relations (HR, Business Development)
    3) Management of unpredictable tasks (CEO)

F) THE DANGER OF SPECIALISING

"I can probably earn more in an hour of writing or even teaching than I could save in a whole week of cooking. Specialization is undeniably a powerful social and economic force. And yet it is also debilitating. It breeds helplessness, dependence, and ignorance and, eventually, it undermines any sense of responsibility."
Michael Pollan – Author

Our Innovation Director was adamant that developers could not be replaced by computers, but a CEO could. I responded in the same way as most employees: "My job can't be replaced by a computer!" Whether I was correct or not, acting as an ostrich and assuming that a job cannot be replaced by a computer will lead slowly but surely to a loss of that job – to the competition. Somewhere, either around the corner or across the world, another company will be working out how to automate tasks that will make their product cheaper and probably better than yours.

Each modern-day job consists of a series of tasks – some of which can be more easily replicated by computers than others. This is summarised in the table below.

Table 2.2 The Effect of AI on Office Jobs

Office Job	Effect from Artificial Intelligence
Computer Programmer	Computers are already starting to write code that will replace programmers. By devising AI programs computer programmers will write themselves out of a job. However, programmers who understand business requirements will still be required to write test code.
Customer Support Agent	Voice recognition, continuously learning knowledge bases and automated voice responses (from knowledge bases) will remove the need for customer support agents.
Bookkeeper and Accountant	Most finance tasks can be processed and therefore will be automated. Senior management

	accountants will be needed to bring multiple sources of information together and combine this with Emotional Intelligence.
Lawyer	Already computers can analyse and respond on case law. Smart contracts and blockchain will remove much need for lawyers.
Business Developer	Difficult to replace as each opportunity can be unique and relates across multiple departments. Also uses multiple sources of information, which is costly to program into computers.
Sales Person and Purchaser	Much of sales and purchasing has been and will be more automated using purchasing platforms. Amazon has already changed the future of selling.
Marketeer	Too many different roles to be able to generalise. Marketing initiative will be required to try new methods and ideas. Other jobs which can be processed (including content writing or lead generation) will be automated.
Operations Manager	The role of operations is to create and fulfil processes – these should be automated. Operations manager will be required only to automate new processes
Humans Resources Manager	HR processes (payroll etc.) will be automated. A good HR Director focused on building or maintaining the company culture will have value.
CEO	CEO has to deal with a lot of different tasks, including pushing people to keep momentum. AI will help with strategic decision-making. CEO should aim to become redundant by pushing ownership and responsibility down the organisation.

Chapter 3

BUSINESS CHANGE

"The underlying source of anguish for many people in work today is an antiquated system of employment and management designed for an industrial age."
Richard Donkin – Author

The need for business change is simple – companies must survive and thrive in the face of ongoing competition, which involves handling technological changes as well as attracting and motivating the best staff. Today's workforce expects a different working experience than that provided by many hierarchical organisations and self-management provides a preferable environment.

A) SELF-MANAGEMENT

"Humility is what makes teams great."
Rick Pitino – Basketball coach

As outlined in Chapter 1, most organisations are dictatorships and their long-term future is dependent upon the strategic decision-making abilities of the CEO. When companies do not thrive, despite generating revenue, their failure is usually caused by the CEO not understanding, or not responding to, the need for change. I have certainly been slow to react to strategic necessity in the past and I now realise that, for an organisation to be successful, it must not depend upon the CEO alone but, rather, each and every person should provide initiative.

This can be facilitated within self-management. Whilst every organisation has its own culture and personalities and is therefore unique, a key part of any flat organisation is smaller teams which avoid inertia and the 'not my job' attitude found in large groups.

Deciding the size of a team will depend upon three questions:

- What is the objective of the team?
- What skills are needed to achieve that objective?
- Which and how many people are needed to cover those skills?

The way in which teams are created and organised depends largely upon the dynamics of each company. The methodology that we have started to use within Pod Group is covered in Chapter 6.

Having created more manageable groups, flat organisations need varying levels of reporting and decision-making – generally depending upon the level of self-management that teams are given. Let's take each of these in turn.

Reporting can be done for informational or control reasons. If a team is reporting to one or a series of bosses, in positions higher than all the individuals in the team, it will probably be used as battering rams for the bosses to question how the group is working. If, however, the reports are disseminated across, not up and down, the organisation, especially to parallel teams who need the information to complete their work, then they can be valuable.

The way that decisions are made can be similar to and linked to the reporting process (especially in a hierarchical organisation). Alternatively, decision-making can be a separate process that takes place within a team but does not relate to the reporting of activities to other teams.

A number of companies around the world have embraced the concept of totally self-managing teams, which fulfil all the functions of a normal hierarchical organisation. WL Gore, started in 1958, has 9,000 employees across thirty countries. Known for its Gore-Tex products, it has evolved into many other businesses. Its founder, Bill Gore, when he started the company, envisaged a flat structure with autonomous teams making all the decisions required to run their unit. WL Gore uses many processes to stay successful, but one of the most fundamental is that no part of the organisation can grow beyond 200 people.

Self-managed teams are more about the approach and thought process behind work than the structure; and herein lies the problem – it can seem very ambiguous. However, a number of aspects are common amongst all self-managed teams. The first and most important is that bosses need to allow their employees make their own decisions.

As mentioned earlier, this requires a basic assumption that people are good and, if trusted to do so, will generally try and do their best.

Not only does the CEO need to let others make decisions, middle managers also need to let go and this is often even harder to achieve. When their role is usurped, the middle managers' existence is called into question. Their value in the team then comes not from their position, *per se*, but from what they can add. This explains why so many managers leave companies after they become self-managed.

By removing the traditional managerial role, a level of self-motivation is required in each participant of the team to bring out the best in themselves and others. There are no orders to follow, so experience and initiative are required to work out what needs to be done. Training can be an important aspect of self-managed teams where individuals are taught not only the functional aspects of their jobs, but also the soft skills required to work with others. As a result, members of the team are likely to be more motivated and responsible for the work that they are doing.

If each person of the team shows responsibility, an environment of trust in others will be created, where members of the team feel confident to seek and give advice on subjects of which they may have less or more experience.

For self-managed teams to operate effectively, there are two additional requirements. Firstly, the team must understand the values, goals and objectives of the company. Secondly, transparency of all information is necessary; teams need access to all the relevant information to allow for proper decisions, otherwise they may have to refer to another person to provide a decision (or even advice) which limits the functioning of that team.

The inspiration for our change process was Ricardo Semler who wrote 'Maverick' followed by 'Seven Day Weekend' - which is an even better read.

In 1980, Semler took over his father's business (Semco) which supplied products to the shipbuilding business in Brazil. Semco has since grown from a revenue of $4 million to multiple hundreds of millions and from 100 to more than 3,000 employees.

In its early days, Semco was operating in a very industrialised and unionised environment – to the extent that toilet breaks for employees were monitored. As Semler observed, the workers are running their own households and are responsible for their children – and yet we tell them when they can go to the toilet. Semler has removed policy after policy to provide an environment that is run by the employees; and now, despite being the majority owner, he has no say in how the business is run.

The company has three layers of management; provides all information (including financial information) to all employees; leaves employees to choose their own salaries, decide where and how they want to work and which work they want to do; and has eliminated all controls that inhibit employees' ability to get on with their job.

It has been run as a profit-making organisation with double-digit annual growth. Forty years on it is one of Brazil's most successful companies and, more importantly, most desirable companies to work for. Semler's books contain a number of observations that are worth keeping in mind when thinking about the best way to encourage self-management.

The first is around trust and the effect of peers. He removed internal controls and auditing – giving people the responsibility for their own behaviour. However, self-control is enhanced by the knowledge that you are accountable to your peers. There will always be some who abuse the system, but it is not worth creating controls on 100% of the people to avoid the 2% who cause problems. A few will find the flexibility of such a working environment difficult to embrace but employee satisfaction rises as each individual discovers what it takes to do their job.

The second is around decision-making. Decisions take longer in a self-managing environment because the process involves seeking advice from those who would be affected. However implementation is quicker because objections are overcome during this process; and if mistakes are made, they are used to learn, rather than to pass blame.

For me, Semler's most interesting observation is that self-management is self-interest at work. People who are motivated by self-interest will find solutions that no one else can visualise. By putting the priorities of the individual first, the team and eventually the company can profit by fantastically motivated employees.

Aside from Semco, there are a number of inspirational organisations with different levels of self-management, including health-organisations (Buurtzorg in the Netherlands), schools (ESBZ in Germany) and huge multi-nationals. For other examples, it is worth reading Frederic Laloux's book *Reinventing Organisations.*

So, what are the advantages of self-management?

First of all, decision-making. By avoiding the need to refer to others (maybe a lot further) up the chain, decisions are more likely to relate to the actual, not perceived, issue at hand.

I am a firm believer that the majority of the people with whom I work know more than I do about their area of expertise and so their decisions will be more informed than mine.

Often I go through the following type of conversation with new employees (in this case with a system administrator).

Him: "We need more Cloud hosting."

Me: "Right"

Him: "I think we should get more from AWS."

Me: "Right"

Him: "We need this amount."

Me: "Right"

Him: "It will cost this amount."

Me: "Right"

Him: "Can I do it?"

Me: "Are you aware what you are doing now?"

Him: "Eh?"

Me: "You are asking me to make a decision on something about which I have no idea, have no idea of competitive costs and don't know how well it will work. You are better equipped than me to answer this question and yet you want me to take the responsibility for a decision you want to take."

Him: "Umm, so can I do it?"

Me: "I don't know – should you?"

At which point we generally do a repeat of the last two sentences a few times until they go off confused and are subsequently enlightened by a colleague. That enlightenment is simple: "If you know what you should do, then do it."

By being encouraged to make their own decisions, employees are far more likely to take initiative, leading to greater productivity and improved team working.

This improvement in productivity and feeling of responsibility has a direct correlation with improved customer satisfaction. Self-managed teams see improved sales figures and customer service, but where they really excel is in reducing returned products. By taking responsibility in the first place, individuals and teams make sure that mistakes and inferior products are avoided.

This in turn leads to substantial cost savings which can be more significant than increased sales, which will falter anyway if a company gets a reputation for unreliable products.

The cost of stress on a business is often overlooked. When employees are in control of their own destinies, they are less stressed and it also reduces the stress of a CEO. It is no longer necessary to be spinning a story to employees – they already know the truth and the number of decisions that need to be made reduces to almost zero. This leaves the CEO to concentrate on the parts of the job where they can add value. This is certainly true in my case (which is the only reason I could find time to write this book).

A side effect of all of the above is improved communication and scalability.

B) COMMUNICATION & SCALABILITY

"We have two ears and one mouth so that we can listen twice as much as we speak."
Epictetus – Greek Philosopher

Picture a late 19th century office. It would be full of people from the same country, with a clear pecking order, male, same working hours and all speaking the same language. Communication with the outside was in person or by letter. As a result, communication was fairly easy.

Today people could be in the office or working at home, located in different countries, speaking different languages with different cultural references. Naturally there is huge potential for being misunderstood through any of the numerous (and intended to be brief) modes to write to each to other.

One of the key components of communication, and central to the WEIRD methodology, is the giving and taking of advice. This can avoid bias and self-serving agendas. If advice is requested, the adviser is in a powerful position – empowering others to act and influencing decisions. Most importantly, both sides can learn a lot by listening.

According to a Microsoft survey in Canada, the average person has an eight second attention span (down from twelve seconds in 2000).[i]

I have noticed that my listening is oriented to knowing the important facts in as short period of time as possible. Understandably, with the hectic, chaotic, complicated pace of work life today, people are even more committed to getting their own agenda accomplished."[ii]

An article in the online newsletter Fast Company set out six ways to become a better listener which are easily forgotten:

1) Listen to learn, not to be polite;
2) Quiet your own agenda and listen to what someone else is trying to say;
3) Ask more questions;

4) Pay attention to your listen/talk ratio;
5) Repeat back what you heard;
6) Wait until somebody has finished talking before you respond.

Listening is a key part of the advice process; we all assume that we know how to give and take advice, but we would probably all gain from being taught how to both impart and receive advice better.

Giving advice, i.e. asking people to change, as well as taking advice and implementing it, require Emotional Intelligence, self-awareness, restraint, diplomacy and patience.[iii]

We have certainly seen this during the change process in our company. Persuading people to accept the idea of change and to revise their approach to it has been the hardest step. However, various management systems, including the WEIRD methodology described in this book, can help that process.

The key is to split into small enough groups to allow for better one-to-one communication and to break down the barriers created by people focusing only on their specialism. By forming teams that are cross-departmental, each individual has a better understanding of other people's roles A coordinator can communicate with other teams when necessary but the need for this is reduced as each team includes the skills required to run as an autonomous unit. The need for more layers to ensure communication and controls are in place has been eliminated. At this point the issue of scaling can be addressed.

The tendency for any growing organisation is to add more management, communication channels and processes. However, it is always worth asking the question: why is it necessary? At which point it may become clear that these extra layers are not required or that different steps are preferable. It is equally important to look at established ways of doing things and eradicate those that are no longer fit for purpose.

One of the advantages of organic growth is that it is easier to assimilate new employees. A very fast-growing company will find that new employees have not had enough quality time with those in the organisation who are already familiar with the company culture. As a result the culture, core values and trust between colleagues will be diluted, making it harder to overcome problems that arise. Therefore, it is essential to take time to find the right people and make sure that they learn the right mindset, in order to set the stage for speedy and effective scaling along the road.

However, effective scaling should always focus on the core business. Outsourcing other areas will increase capacity without the difficulties of managing more resources internally. Having done this, and automated as much as possible, the desire to scale should, ideally, come from lower down the organisation rather than an ambition from above.

Finally, before scaling, it is important that the business is running without day-to-day input from the CEO who should be able to leave the organisation for a month with no detrimental effect. Unless this is possible, adding more scale increases complications, which will result in a loss of customers to competitors.

C) COMPETITION

"A merchant who approaches business with the idea of serving the public well has nothing to fear from the competition."
James Cash Penney – Founder of JC Penney stores

Much can be said about competition and the need to know what the competition is doing and how you can beat rivals. My viewpoint is controversial and many will disagree with me.

The threat of competition is only that – a threat. Although it is worth knowing what the competition is doing, there is no value in spending time worrying about it.

Making changes as a defensive measure against a potential threat will lead to failure. A football team can't win a game by focusing all its efforts on defending the goal. At some point somebody in the team has to score a goal. That said, the commercial world has become so globalised that it is fair to assume that somebody, somewhere, will be two steps ahead of you. This isn't necessarily a problem, as the flip side of a globalised world is a bigger market – so you can still succeed.

The best way to succeed in the face of competition is to do the best you can. Daniel Priestley in his book *Oversubscribed* encourages entrepreneurs to concentrate on a niche area and become the predominant supplier and leader within that niche. He focuses on changing mindsets to persuade customers that they should be lining up to buy your products. As with most things it is easier said than done, but really comes down to one thing – differentiating yourself from your competition and doing what you do really well, allowing you to build a reputation that will make it almost impossible for others to compete.

There are, however, some useful things that can be learnt from the competition – or lack of competition. If you are starting a new company and cannot find any competition, you may want to re-consider whether there is a market at all.

Assuming that there is competition, this can provide valuable insight as to not only where the market is going, but also the products currently available. Knowing the USPs of each competitor also makes it easier to explain to a potential customer why your product's USPs are better. Most of the effort of competitor analysis should be focused on nimble companies – these are the ones who are more likely to neutralise your advantages.

Finally, it is also necessary to look at those who may not be direct competitors but could provide the same product as yourself. A good example is Amazon which, by adding a new product line, could decimate a smaller company which cannot pivot quickly.

It is not possible to look at the business challenges we face in the next fifteen years without taking into consideration how Artificial Intelligence and disruptive technologies are also going to affect the wider society. This is covered in the next chapter.

Chapter 4

SOCIAL CHANGE

"You never change things by fighting the existing reality. To change something, build a new model that makes the existing model obsolete."

Richard Buckminster Fuller – American architect

A) THE PURPOSE OF WORK AND LIFE

"Achievement of your happiness is the only moral purpose of your life, and that happiness, not pain or mindless self-indulgence, is the proof of your moral integrity, since it is the proof and the result of your loyalty to the achievement of your values."
Ayn Rand – Author

Our satisfaction in life is intrinsically tied up with our health and wider social factors. Despite the constant barrage of negative news given to us by the media, we actually live in a far better world than in any period of human history. In his book *Factfulness: Ten Reasons We're Wrong About the World – and Why Things Are Better Than You Think*, Hans Rosling proves how outdated and negative our perception of worldwide health and social factors is. He starts his book with a quiz to give us a sense of our understanding of the state of the world. My answers were better than the chimpanzees he uses as a base line to compare our level of knowledge – but not by much. Mind you I still did better than most politicians.

We tend to rely on historic rather than current facts. As Rosling pointed out, children are taught by teachers who still rely on facts that are often thirty years out of date. We remember big events, but don't notice the small changes happening each day which change the world. Our perception is that each industrial revolution improved our quality of life. In reality, although industrial revolutions have changed industry, they have not necessarily improved working lives (changing from manual work in the field to manual work in the factory did not improve working conditions). However, industrial and technological changes, combined with social changes implemented over the last two hundred years, have revolutionised the way we live – with health and social care that our ancestors could not even envisage. The number of people in the world living in poverty has been falling steadily for generations.

However, it is only today at the start of the fourth industrial revolution that technology is allowing us to change our attitude towards office work, insomuch as roles and place of work have become less important and flexibility of working becomes easier.

Until approximately thirty years ago, for the majority of people, work was not to be enjoyed but endured (and for many people holding down multiple jobs in order to survive, I accept that the situation is still the same).

However, for those of us lucky enough to have choice about the work we do, there is an interesting question as to whether work is just a means of survival or a purpose in itself. According to theoretical physicist and author Stephen Hawking, "Work gives you meaning and purpose and life is empty without it." With a French influence in my family, I have found that there are significant differences in attitudes to work between the Anglo-Saxon mentality and the continental European mentality. Brought up in an Anglo-Saxon culture, from my perspective, work needs to be as fulfilling as possible. Part of the French side of my family sees work as a means to enjoy holidays and leisure time. That is not to say that they don't want fulfilling work – but it isn't their first priority.

Aside from cultural differences, there are also generational differences. I was born into Generation X and we feel that we should be working hard, but also enjoying our family. Often, we end up doing neither well.

A study by EY in 2016 looked at the attitudes of different generations towards work in the US .[i] The most interesting result was the difference in attitudes in older millennials compared to younger millennials and Generation Z.

When questioned about job satisfaction or career goals, older millennials scored considerably higher than other generations on the need for freedom to dress as they want, work in an open environment, have their own office, have the option to work remotely, be reimbursed for tuition costs and have bonuses adapted to their performance. In terms of salaries and compensation, the younger Millennials and Generation Z have similar expectations to those of Generation X. However, the older millennials have expectations of approximately 20% higher salaries.

An obvious improvement in our working lives is our understanding of the need for equality for women in the workplace. Strangely, in the millennial generation, the gap between women and men was highest for the desire to achieve a high salary, position or leadership (with men wanting more) compared to every other generation. Why this is, I am not sure, but Generation Z view gender equality as a non-negotiable right, so I would hope that this difference is due to a positive choice by women rather than a glass ceiling.

Over the last 70 years, soft benefits have entered the working person's consciousness, such that these are now key to the choice of employment. The EY study shows this for the three youngest generations.

Top three benefits wanted from employees:

Generation Z	Younger Millennials	Older Millennials
Health Insurance coverage	Feeling my ideas are valued	Health Insurance coverage
Feeling my ideas are valued	Health Insurance coverage	Work-life balance
Recognition for my contribution	Work-life balance	Vacation/paid time off

This study shows that, as the new generations enter the work force, they expect to be able to add, and be recognised for, their value. To achieve this, it is necessary to push ownership and responsibility down the ladder by the implementation of WEIRD practices (Wisdom, Emotional intelligence, Initiative, Responsibility, Development [self]).

This will help us to overcome the technological changes of the next fifteen years and beyond. It is ironic that, having finally reached a point where people have choices around how and on what they want to work, that choice could be taken away by the technology that made it possible. Technology has already changed our way of working, but the introduction of Artificial Intelligence is the elephant in the room that cannot be ignored.

Its future impact is, of course, unknown, but Artificial Intelligence requires data. However, it is not clear is from a social standpoint who will control ownership of the data and therefore own the output of any Artificial Intelligence programs?

B) WHO OWNS THE DATA IN A DATA DRIVEN WORLD?

"Those who rule data will rule the entire world."
Masayoshi Son – CEO Softbank

The value of computers is not in their processors, but rather in the data that they collect. Likewise, the value of many companies is now based on their ability to use data that they collect. The appetite for data appears to be insatiable – 90% of information ever produced has been generated in the last two years.[ii] This trend is not going to slow down as more data are collected to provide personalised advertising, social media, medical treatments – in fact all aspects of our life. It is not the computers demanding this information, but the designers of the software that encourage us to provide data (willingly or unknowingly). This can then be processed as part of a bigger data set in order to draw conclusions that may not be true – or may be more perceptive than we would care to admit.

Yuval Noah Harari in his excellent 2015 book *Homo Deus: A Brief History of Tomorrow* talks about the Internet of All Things, focused around the belief of the truth of data.[iii] He gives an example of how Facebook may know you better than anybody knows you – including your spouse. Facebook asked 86,220 volunteers one hundred questions about themselves. Based on the analysis of only 10 'likes', Facebook could always predict each recipient's answers better than a work colleague. After 70 'likes', Facebook produced better predictions of the recipient's answers than friends; 150 'likes' beat family members and 300 'likes' beat spouses. So, if we have more than 300 'likes' on our Facebook account – then advice from Facebook will be more reflective of our personality than any human advice, including that from our partner. This brings a new angle to an adolescent blaming a friend for getting in trouble – "but Facebook said I should do it".

My children are doing most of their learning at school on computers. As far as I know, each piece of work is not being recorded in an ever-growing database about their life. But it wouldn't be difficult to do. If it were recorded throughout their time at school, there would be a huge database that not only provides a progression of their education but could also give a very accurate assessment of how their character and thoughts have matured over the years. Add that to the children's genome sequence, Facebook personality assessment and their web searches and the result is a mountain of data.

If all the data were fed into some larger databases of other children, and continued into adulthood, then the addition of some Machine Learning could produce a very accurate prediction of the type of job they would excel at and an excellent profile to provide to a dating app to find their perfect mate. But would a dating app with all this information be better than relying on romanticism?

The philosopher Alan de Botton in a talk on Romanticism[iv] pointed out the danger of the modern-day concept of a marriage based on romanticism which replaced the marriage of reason around 1750. Romanticism puts much emphasis of choosing a partner because instinctively it feels right. This compares to a relationship of reason based on, for example, neighbouring land. Many of these historic marriages of reason were a disaster (normally for the women), but could a matching app (which is the modern-day equivalent of overly zealous parents) be more successful than relying on the instinctive choice? As a product of the romantic marriage era, I have a belief in human irrational behaviour. However, my scientific side says exactly that – it is irrational, inefficient and a poor way to make a decision. Why, with all the data available, would the next generation choose to make instinctive decisions?

Yuval Harari explores the viewpoint of 'dataism' believers – those who worship data over any other God, envisaging an all-encompassing cosmic data processing system that will cause Homo sapiens not to exist in its current form but as a super-human race. This would seem rather futuristic, but if we take the processed data mentioned above and find a way to incorporate it into our brain to use in daily life – we would be closer to self-awareness than anybody in the history of man. But who would own the data?

As we move towards a scenario where almost everything will provide data, the opportunity for creating efficiencies is huge. As an example, aggregated health data will result in personalised medicine, which will create incentives for the medical profession to focus on prevention rather than cure – thus saving huge amounts of money as well as lives.

An individual's health data alone is of limited value to others. But once it is joined with data from thousands of others, valuable trends begin to emerge.

23andMe provides DNA analysis for anybody who wants to research their lineage. For $99 and a saliva sample, the company can provide the details of your forefathers. It is now one of a handful of health companies with a valuation of over $1 billion but this value is not in the 'know your ancestor service' – but in the fact that people are voluntarily sending their saliva to be tested for DNA. To be fair to the company, they appear to have a very strict opt-in policy regarding the use of the DNA for other research purposes – but apparently 80% of people do opt in. This allows the company to sell the data to pharmaceutical companies. If this is then used to aid the development of better drugs, it could be argued that it's a good thing. However, it is clear that the data do not remain personal.

So when does a good thing veer on the side of evil? As has already happened with the collection of consumer data, there is a tipping point after which it is difficult to compete with the existing holders of Big Data.

I was asked by a Silicon Valley lawyer whether our company was pre- or post-revenue? I understood the words but couldn't understand why a company would want to be pre-revenue – isn't the point of companies to sell things? Not necessarily! Well-funded start-ups are grabbing customers, regardless of the cost, in the hope that the data gained will more than pay back the cost of acquiring these customers. The dream of many new start-ups is to find a niche outside the interest of Google, Apple, Facebook or Amazon and to grow a sufficient customer base of data to then be bought by one of these companies. It is this approach to building companies that makes it extremely difficult for revenue-creating, organically grown companies to survive and why the lure of investors with deep pockets allowing companies to buy customers (or data) is so hard to resist.

But how can these companies say they own the data? Similar to 23andMe, in the use of various services we agree to allow our data to be used for other purposes. In theory, it may be possible to opt out, but in so doing so we limit what we can and can't do online. When pushed, the likes of Facebook will resort to the argument that if people don't want their data to be used, they can stop using Facebook. However, for many, this would restrict their social life severely. For some teenagers, stopping Instagram (owned by Facebook) could result in exclusion or bullying at school. Thus, these four companies have reached a tipping point where it is almost impossible for others to compete.

They have huge amounts of data on millions of individuals that they use for their own profit.[v] Further, they have created an exclusive ownership class from which they can create an array of more and more efficient services by using Artificial Intelligence to mine the data that they hold.

Considering that these services will make our lives more efficient, and thus we will want to buy them, how do we stop this being used to the detriment of the consumer?

C) THE LITIGATION & REGULATION PARADOX

"Success in creating AI would be the biggest event in human history. Unfortunately, it might also be the last, unless we learn how to avoid the risks."
Stephen Hawking – Theoretical Physicist

As mentioned above, we are moving into an era where those who hold the data could potentially control, or at least influence, much of our lives with the use of Artificial Intelligence programs. To date computer programs are passive; the worry of Artificial Intelligence is that it can make them active.

In July 2017, Elon Musk said, "Artificial Intelligence is a fundamental risk to the existence of human civilisation." He added that Artificial Intelligence is one of the most pressing threats to the survival of the human race.[vi] So, should it be regulated?

In January 2017 in Asilomar, California, a set of 23 principles were formulated in the hope of ensuring Artificial Intelligence is used beneficially for human kind. More than 1,200 Artificial Intelligence researchers signed up to adhere to the Asilomar principles.[vii] Despite his alarmist statements, Musk's main point is that Artificial Intelligence is advancing so fast that governments should get involved now to avoid scary scenarios wittingly or unwittingly created by programmers, rather than act with knee-jerk legislation later.

Some of the Asilomar principles include:

- Science–Policy Link: There should be constructive and healthy exchange between Artificial Intelligence researchers and policy makers.
- Research Culture: A culture of cooperation, trust and transparency should be fostered among researchers and developers of Artificial Intelligence.

- Race Avoidance: Teams developing Artificial Intelligence systems should actively cooperate to avoid corner cutting on safety standards.
- Importance: Advanced Artificial Intelligence could represent a profound change in the history of life on earth and should be planned for and managed with commensurate care and resources.
- Risks: Risks posed by Artificial Intelligence systems, especially catastrophic or existential risks, must be subject to planning and mitigation efforts commensurate with their expected impact.

So far, so nice. Within the Asilomar principles, there is a sub-section regarding ethics and values.

- Human Values: Artificial Intelligence systems should be designed and operated so as to be compatible with ideals of human dignity, rights, freedoms and cultural diversity.
- Human Control: Humans should choose how and whether to delegate decisions to Artificial Intelligence systems, to accomplish human-chosen objectives.

The full Asilomar Principles are given overleaf.

Table 4.1: The full Asilomar Principles:

GOAL	DESCRIPTION
Research	
Research Goal	The goal of AI research should be to create not undirected intelligence, but beneficial intelligence.
Research Funding	Investments in AI should be accompanied by funding for research on ensuring its beneficial use, including thorny questions in computer science, economics, law, ethics and social studies; such as: • How can we make future AI systems highly robust, so that they do what we want without malfunctioning or getting hacked? • How can we grow our prosperity through automation while maintaining people's resources and purpose? • How can we update our legal systems to be more fair and efficient, to keep pace with AI, and to manage the risks associated with AI? • What set of values should AI be aligned with, and what legal and ethical status should it have?
Science–Policy Link	There should be constructive and healthy exchange between AI researchers and policy-makers.
Research Culture	A culture of cooperation, trust, and transparency should be fostered among researchers and developers of AI.
Race Avoidance	Teams developing AI systems should actively cooperate to avoid corner-cutting on safety standards.

Ethics and Values	
Safety	AI systems should be safe and secure throughout their operational lifetime, and verifiably so where applicable and feasible.
Failure Transparency	If an AI system causes harm, it should be possible to ascertain why.
Judicial Transparency	Any involvement by an autonomous system in judicial decision-making should provide a satisfactory explanation auditable by a competent human authority.
Responsibility	Designers and builders of advanced AI systems are stakeholders in the moral implications of their use, misuse and actions, with a responsibility and opportunity to shape those implications.
Value Alignment	Highly autonomous AI systems should be designed so that their goals and behaviours can be assured to align with human values throughout their operation.
Human Values	AI systems should be designed and operated so as to be compatible with ideals of human dignity, rights, freedoms and cultural diversity.
Personal Privacy	People should have the right to access, manage and control the data they generate, given AI systems' power to analyse and utilize that data.
Liberty and Privacy	The application of AI to personal data must not unreasonably curtail people's real or perceived liberty.
Shared Benefit	AI technologies should benefit and empower as many people as possible.
Shared Prosperity	The economic prosperity created by AI should be shared broadly, to benefit all of humanity.

Human Control	Humans should choose how and whether to delegate decisions to AI systems, to accomplish human-chosen objectives.
Non-subversion	The power conferred by control of highly advanced AI systems should respect and improve, rather than subvert, the social and civic processes on which the health of society depends.
AI Arms Race	An arms race in lethal autonomous weapons should be avoided.
Longer-term Issues	
Capability Caution	There being no consensus, we should avoid strong assumptions regarding upper limits on future AI capabilities.
Importance	Advanced AI could represent a profound change in the history of life on Earth, and should be planned for and managed with commensurate care and resources.
Risks	Risks posed by AI systems, especially catastrophic or existential risks, must be subject to planning and mitigation efforts commensurate with their expected impact.
Recursive Self-Improvement	AI systems designed to recursively self-improve or self-replicate in a manner that could lead to rapidly increasing quality or quantity must be subject to strict safety and control measures.
Common Good	Superintelligence should only be developed in the service of widely shared ethical ideals, and for the benefit of all humanity rather than one state or organisation.

I mentioned the modern-day philosopher, Alan de Botton previously, and defining these human values will provide plenty of material for him and other philosophers over the next few years. These philosophers are better equipped to define these human values than I am, so this book focuses on one of the questions asked within the Asilomar principles: "How can we grow our prosperity through automation whilst maintaining people's resources and purpose?" The question of human purpose is a huge sociological challenge that we face over the next fifteen years.

The advocates of the Asilomar principles call for regulation. However, one of the drawbacks of over-regulation is that it stifles innovation.[viii] As the implications of Artificial Intelligence are relatively unknown, few governments are willing to be enthusiastic about regulating its use; firstly because it is not clear what should be regulated and secondly because governments fear that regulation will move research and jobs to other less regulated territories. Indeed, there will be a tendency to enact laws that will protect jobs which would otherwise be replaced by Artificial Intelligence. This, in my view, would be a mistake; better that we appreciate early that the future of work will change and prepare for the social implications of this fourth industrial revolution.

Part of the solution is a different approach to law. At present, companies try to control everything and anything so as to avoid being sued. The result of this is often absurd rules and processes that dampen any initiative that an employee could show.

We need to create an environment that allows employees to take ownership of what they are doing but protects them and the company from court cases as a result of decisions that may not have been wise?

Over the years, I have found that the best way to avoid the possibility of a court case is to be ready to provide a genuine apology, even if not entirely at fault, and to keep communicating in order to understand why the other party is hurt.

In the future, legal uncertainty will be largely avoided due to smart contracts which will ensure that an action follows an event without human interaction. With this in place, the vagaries of a contract and human interpretation become irrelevant – if the event takes place then the action happens and vice versa.

However, in the meantime, company rules may be absurd to one person but sensible to another. If employees are given the freedom to take ownership of their tasks and take what they perceive to be the best decisions, then there needs to be an understanding of what is absurd and what is sensible. Making people go on training courses just so that a training box can be ticked is not going to provide benefits in the long term. However, motivating employees to want to go on courses that consider the legal aspects of their job is a great start. If you encourage people to use common sense instead of trying to second-guess what their boss would do, then they will probably do the right thing – and become wiser as a result.

Wisdom is generally learnt through experience which brings the knowledge to avoid doing things that may result in being sued. So how else can you impart this knowledge?

The advice process is a very effective way to resolve this predicament. Decision makers should be looking at the financial, personnel, social, organisational and other aspects of any decision – making sure that it makes sense legally is part of that consideration. Therefore, advice givers should encourage decision makers to consider the legal aspect of any decision alongside the more fun stuff.

Although we need to be careful not to encourage a more litigious society, the social implications of automation, especially as a result of the effects of Artificial Intelligence, are probably of more concern.

D) SOCIAL IMPLICATIONS OF AUTOMATION

"Automation is great for profits, but it's a real potential trouble area for society."
Chieh Huang – Boxed CEO

"Managed badly, the benefits of automation could be narrowly concentrated, benefiting those who own capital and highly skilled workers. Inequality would spiral." – Institute for Public Policy Research[ix]

The IPPR report makes various suggestions to politicians. These include: re-training programmes; an ethics watchdog to oversee the use of automating technologies; new models of company ownership; forcing businesses over a certain size to share profits with workers; and the creation of a sovereign fund to invest in businesses.

However, it is not only the implications of automation that could cause upheavals in society. Other factors combined with automation could leave part (possibly the majority) of society disenfranchised. These include:

- Growth in low skilled jobs (as more people become available to undertake these jobs, the pay for these jobs will decrease).
- Proportionally less working people as we are surviving longer.
- Greater change in monthly incomes leading to uncertainty.
- Increased numbers of people on zero-hour contracts. This allows employers to choose when and if they need people to work.
- An increase in the length of time it takes for the unemployed to find a new job. This leads to an increasingly de-skilled and de-motivated part of the workforce.

In addition to these points, some countries, especially the UK, are in the middle of a confidence crisis about productivity. The UK scores

18% below the productivity average of OECD countries. Since the 2008 financial crises, almost all countries are below their previous productivity levels. Sir Howard Davies, Chairman of the Royal Bank of Scotland, commented "It would seem that, in addition to the factors affecting all developed economies, the UK has particularly weak management."[x]

Leaving the UK's problems aside, the upheavals expected in the future will result in calls to regulate and protect jobs. On the surface this may seem like a sensible move considering how quickly society will have to adjust to mass redundancies. The trouble with this approach is that companies in other countries who have automated successfully will provide a better service and cheaper products than in countries where jobs are being protected artificially. Trade barriers could be raised (as they have already for other reasons) but these will cause export markets to be closed in retaliation – and the downward spiral starts.

However, in my opinion, the worst thing about artificially protecting jobs that are repetitive in nature is that it delays the inevitable and sucks the spirit out of those working in those industries. One of our offices is in Andalusia, Spain. It is frustrating dealing with the Andalusian administration as it appears that jobs are maintained and created regardless of whether they are required. This creates employee disenchantment which results in poor service.

For those who do not accept the change that technology will bring, an anti-technology movement will arise over the next few years. This movement will be like the luddites who destroyed looms in the industrial revolution – and may become as violent.

Unless we find a third way, we will have either a large unemployed group of society bitter about the onset of Artificial Intelligence or a large disillusioned swathe of society in protected jobs. Both scenarios will result in a mass of restless and unhappy people.

The most likely scenario is an ever-decreasing number of people with jobs. As more and more jobs become processed, and therefore replaced by a computer, unemployment will increase. This will cause a downward pressure on existing salaries. The only good thing about a decrease in salaries is that job losses will slow for a while because it will be cheaper to employ people than to rely on automation. However, innovation will continue its march forward and at some point, the use of computers will again become more cost effective than using people.

There is an argument that workers need to be compensated differently, perhaps by becoming part of the ownership class. Various countries (such as Germany) have or are pushing legislation to encourage this. However, this does not necessarily solve the problem – even if workers become owners, if there are no workers employed, there are no workers to be owners.

This will create envy against those with a job. Those who can add value above that provided by a computer will continue to be employed. However, those who will benefit most are the owners of companies that become more and more efficient and profitable – mainly by automating more and cutting jobs.

Or would they? If you own a company making products or selling services, there is one thing that you need. Buyers. Removing a working class also removes a consumer class. Ford understood this when he paid his workers sufficient such that they could eventually become buyers of the Ford motor car.

If you remove the consumer class, then companies that make products, profit and therefore pay taxes will eventually end up with no customers, no profit and pay no taxes. At this point there is no money in the government coffers to provide services for those who are unemployed and need to survive. Under our existing method of capitalism, it is therefore vital that, however it receives the money, a consumer class continues to exist.

With 3D printing and the ability to sell globally, one option for increasing employment is the creation of cottage industries to provide bespoke goods and services – anything from a one-off shirt to an individualised medical device or provision of entertainment services for elderly people in retirement homes. Human beings have huge initiative and creative ideas – the problem is providing an environment to put those ideas in practice.

Step forward the Universal Basic Income.

E) UNIVERSAL BASIC INCOME

"Basic Income is not a utopia, it's a practical business plan for the next step of the human journey"
Jeremy Rifkin – Economic and Social Theorist

The Universal Basic Income (UBI or Basic Income Guarantee) was originally suggested in the late 1800s in England as an alternative to what we now know as the welfare state. Since then there have been some experiments – but no programme has caught hold. The list of those advocating the UBI is growing and includes Richard Branson, Elon Musk, Mark Zuckerberg and many more Silicon Valley moguls. Various politicians on both the left and the right have skirted around the idea – but politically it is a divisive issue. Think of it another way: despite the overwhelming evidence that reform rather than incarceration reduces re-offending amongst prisoners, few politicians are willing to appear to be soft on criminals. In the same way, they don't want to appear soft on employment issues.

The idea around the UBI is very simple. The state provides a fixed amount to every adult in the country (often with an additional amount for children). A UBI would replace the myriad of welfare benefits that are paid. Welfare payments are complicated, benefit some over others, are open to abuse and cost a lot to manage. The UBI removes this complication and reduces the cost of administrating a welfare system. However, it has never been introduced on a large scale because of two assumptions: 1) it will cost too much; and 2) people are inherently lazy and will therefore choose to stop working.

Regarding the cost, if every adult were to be paid enough to live on, there wouldn't be enough in the government budget to cover this. So, taxes would have to be raised in the hope that the economy would grow sufficiently to cover this. Given that jobs, and therefore economies, could crash over the next 15 years, relying on future tax collection to fund an unknown programme is risky.

However, there are statistics which suggest that it may be worth the risk; for example, a report from the Roosevelt Institute in November 2017 predicted the USA could see a $2.48 trillion increase in the nation's GDP within just eight years if it implemented a UBI.[xi] Various trials have taken place that appear to strongly suggest that the UBI could work.

In 1968, Nixon instigated a trial in which 8,500 people were given a basic income of around $1,600 a year for a family of four (equivalent to $10,000/£8,070 today). However, shortly afterwards he axed the programme having been persuaded by right-wing advisers, quoting a report from the English Royal Commission 150 years earlier that 'proved' UBI to be a failure. Historians have since reviewed the report and found that those who had commissioned the report had pre-determined that as people were perceived to be idle, the scheme would not work. The report writers therefore fixed the results to suit their masters' political goals.

More recently, a trial in Finland has been instigated which pays a guaranteed income to 250 unemployed residents. Similar trials have begun or are starting in Canada, USA, The Netherlands and the UK. Others have taken place in India and Africa. From those that have been completed, feedback has been positive. As people don't have to focus solely on surviving, recipients have the time and motivation to take responsibility for their lives.

The other hindrance to introducing the UBI is the assumption that people are lazy.

In a Gallup conducted poll worldwide asking about attitudes to work, 63% of people were not engaged with their work and a further 24% were actively disengaged,[xii] suggesting that 87% of workers are demotivated at work. This appears to be a worldwide problem which is perhaps slanted more to younger people, especially millennials where two thirds want to change jobs in the next 12 months.[xiii] Disengagement can easily be mistaken for laziness.

Leaving aside the bigger issue of how we motivate people to enjoy their work, trials do not suggest that UBI encourages laziness – in fact the opposite.

Canada ran a trial in the 1970s, giving 30% of the people in the small town of Dauphin, Manitoba, $15,000 each. Analysis of the trial by Evelyn Forget, an economist at the University of Manitoba, found that high school completion rates increased and hospitalisation rates dropped by 8.5%.[xiv] Employment rates amongst adults did not change at all. Similar findings appeared in the Nixon trial before it was stopped, when most of those who received money continued to work similar hours, and when working hours fell, the recipients undertook socially beneficial activities. Nixon's trial also found that young people tended to spend more time in education when they were not working.

So financially, how could this work? Let's take the UK as an example.

Each year in the UK, £114 billion is spent on welfare (including Family & Children, Unemployment, Housing, Social Exclusion and Social Protection). Pensions and health are separate budgets. Twenty-three million people of working age do not pay taxes in the UK – because they earn under £10,000. If this £114 billion were paid out as a UBI to each of these 23 million, it would equate to nearly £5,000 per annum per person. This is more than is currently paid for unemployment benefit and wouldn't have strings attached. It could be more if those whose total earnings already exceed £5,000 received less. Some adjustment may be needed to pay an additional amount for disability and supporting children, but otherwise it is simple compared to the current complicated welfare payment system. Anthony Painter, a director at the RSA think-tank, commented on what would happen if a UBI of just under £4,000 were paid. "By itself, it wouldn't be enough to take someone out of poverty, but it could give them the flexibility to re-train or the breathing room to wait for a job that has prospects rather than being forced into taking the first vacancy that comes along."

And this is the point – the object of the UBI is to remove the link between receiving welfare benefits and proving that you have been looking for a job. The task of (constantly) looking for a job is extremely time consuming and frankly depressing – if unemployment benefit depends upon showing that you have either been looking for or have taken part time jobs, you will be limited in time and motivation to find other ways to generate cash. Alternative employment could include making products (bespoke or otherwise) to sell. Jobs taken in order to survive rarely lead to personal or career development, and this leads to greater depression, more social problems and increased cost on society.

One of the greatest social problems we face today is mental illness – which is also one of the biggest expenditures for public health systems. How much of this is caused by people being forced to do jobs that they hate in order to survive? As shown in the Canadian trial mentioned above, a UBI has the potential to reduce hospital visits and therefore reduce health care costs.

The UK mental health charity – MIND – has calculated that 10% of GDP is lost to stress and sites four aspects at work that contribute to this: poor working conditions; unclear roles; personality factors; and poor relationships. Unfortunately, no company can resolve all these problems for all their workers, but giving more control and responsibility to each individual (whether employed or not) will allow people to take control of their own lives and therefore reduce their own stress.

Godfrey Moase, activist and assistant general branch secretary at the National Union of Workers in Melbourne, Australia, gave a good vision of where UBI could lead. "Imagine the creativity, innovation and enterprise that would be unleashed if every citizen were guaranteed a living", he wrote. "Social enterprises, cooperatives and small businesses could be started without participants worrying where the next pay cheque would come from."

The speed of innovation, whilst leading to a loss of jobs has also led to the creation of the 3D printing machine. Described as the next most important disruptive influence after the internet, 3D printing creates a technological solution for those citizens who wish to unleash their creativity, innovation and enterprise. This will displace jobs from factories as products will be created on a printer at home. By manufacturing locally, waste will be reduced and transportation costs cut.

3D printing is particularly good for creating one-off products. As manufactured goods (mainly from China) become more homogenised, there will be an increased demand for bespoke products. Approximately two thirds of new jobs are created by small businesses. Therefore 3D printing (combined with a different mentality towards employment as set out in this book) provides the opportunity for a myriad of cottage industries to be created. Combine this with the UBI and, instead of spending time looking for meaningless jobs, people could be creating bespoke products to be sold locally or for which the design could be sold to a customer half way around the world.

Allowing people the freedom to think beyond survival and create their own employment would provide a level of satisfaction and self-control far beyond any other job offered by somebody else. It is one of a number of tools that could prepare the world for the future, but we have to start with our children – through a different method of education.

Chapter 5

EDUCATIONAL CHANGE

"Ideally, what should be said to every child, repeatedly, throughout his or her school life is something like this: 'You are in the process of being indoctrinated. We have not yet evolved a method of education that is not a system of indoctrination. We are sorry, but it is the best we can do. What you are being taught here is an amalgam of current prejudice and the choices of this particular culture. The slightest look at history will show how impermanent these must be. You are being taught by people who have been able to accommodate themselves to a regime of thought laid down by their predecessors. It is a self-perpetuating system. Those of you who are more robust and individual than others will be encouraged to leave and find ways of educating yourself – educating your own judgements. Those that stay must remember, always and all the time, that they are being moulded and patterned to fit into the narrow and particular needs of this particular society."

Doris Lessing, The Golden Notebook

A) CHANGING OUR EDUCATIONAL SYSTEM

"Education is the most powerful weapon which you can use to change the world."
Nelson Mandela – Former President of South Africa

Suggesting that people will lose their job to Artificial Intelligence is one level of controversy; suggesting that children should be educated differently is far more emotive.

Likewise, encouraging managers to allow employees to bring out the best of themselves is simple compared to persuading teachers to change the way they teach. Although teachers don't have competitors nipping at their heels, they do have government-set methodologies to follow and try to navigate whilst bringing out the best in each child. These facts ensure that change within schools, both at an administrative and personnel level, is hard.

However, unless we change the way our children are educated, they will not be prepared for a world in which machines carry out repetitive tasks and people carry out the tasks that require versatility.

My own children study in a school that is going through a change process and I have discussed further potential changes with its senior management. New experiments and initiatives have been started – but there is a long way to go. However, the task that they are undertaking is far more complicated than that undertaken by us at Pod Group. Their customers are parents – the majority of whom don't want their children to be guinea pigs in what they perceive may be an ill-fated experiment. Their employees are teachers, many of whom have taught at the school for many years. They see no reason to change what 'works' and certainly don't see any benefits in taking practices from the commercial world.

One of the things that has not changed between my school experience and that of my children is that in both cases we have spent countless hours in lessons achieving and learning nothing. At the end of each year we had gained a certain amount of academic knowledge, but when compared to nine or ten months of full time input – the output is low. Every day I know that each of my children will have attended at least two lessons that were ill suited to their level, and so they would not have paid attention. And therein lies the problem; the current educational system does not capture children's attention.

Life is short and the first 18 (or 21 if you include university) years are an amazing opportunity to get to know lots of interesting things. However, there appears to be an attitude that the goal of education is for children to reach a minimum standard of knowledge by the time they leave school, regardless of different aptitudes and interests.

Whilst controversial, project and personalised learning offer two routes to make education more interesting, increase the time teachers can spend one-on-one with pupils and ensure that learning is focused on the abilities of each child in order to make more efficient use of their time.

Project-based learning

Many schools across the world have implemented project-based learning. Most of the time this has resulted in looking at the curriculum for that year and teachers working together to ensure that the requirements are pulled into a number of projects.

Whilst this is better than creating silos of subjects, it is only a marginal improvement. Working on a project rather than separate disciplines allows students to get a better feel of how these disciplines relate to each other. More importantly, project work is more interesting for students as disciplines are brought into a real-life environment rather than being taught as isolated and theoretical subjects.

Setting up a project-based curriculum requires an enhanced level of trust between teachers. Teaching disciplines separately allows teachers, for the most part, to work solely within their department and coordinate mostly with other teachers specialising in the same discipline. Project-based work requires coordination across disciplines, a basic knowledge of other subjects, trust that the student's time will be shared appropriately and, most of all, a willingness to embrace a harder way to assess results. In short — potentially more work.

However, for as long as basic teaching methods remain the same, even within a project-based system, students are unlikely to be better prepared than they are today.

To address this, two things need to happen:

1) Students need to be more involved in their learning programme and take more ownership of their studies.
2) Curricula and learning methods need to reflect each student's learning abilities, preferred method of learning and understanding at the time. It is impossible for 30 students to have the same interest and ability to master a topic at the same time. Allowing students to learn in different ways, at different times and on different projects (not necessarily split by year) would help each student to gain a knowledge of everything that they should cover by the end of their school years. Furthermore, it allows them to advance beyond the minimum level in disciplines that they find easier.

Now, and for the foreseeable future, there is a huge shortage of data scientists. Computers are great for crunching numbers and finding patterns — but they lack the ability to bring disparate and unrelated thoughts together.

On the surface, a project around data collection and interpretation would seem a very dull project for the average teenager. However, an enthusiastic teacher could devise an interesting project that would incorporate most subjects that they study. For example, by explaining the success of their favourite YouTube idol, social and natural sciences, maths, languages, music, art and technology could all be brought into a project. This could easily be extended to include data analysis on a variety of questions around the subject. The success of such a project would be enhanced by allowing students to work at different speeds and concentrate on different angles.

By moving away from yearly learning targets, students could progress at their own pace. For example, bilingual students would be ahead of the average student in a language and could help others with pronunciation or comprehension in return for assistance in other subjects. This mutual aid would build self-esteem and create a cooperative working environment.

Most of all, by allowing students to work on projects that they find interesting, the ingredient that is so often missing in school – enthusiasm – is added. By allowing children to choose how and what they want to study (within a framework), motivation will be much higher.

Personalised learning

The ability to cover topics by which students are enthused is one of the biggest advantages of personalised learning. It also moves the ownership of each student's studies from the teacher to themselves.

Many (especially teachers and parents of teenagers) would argue that, given the choice, most teenagers would not study. I agree that sometimes they need a verbal kick to get work done, but this is a chicken and egg situation. The more you tell children (or adults) what to do, the less they take the initiative and motivate themselves.

So, what is personalised learning and how can it help? Advanced personalised learning can be split into three different systems increasing in sophistication: Data Driven Learning (comparable to recommendations from Amazon – you understand this, so now you can start this); Adaptive Learning (the program identifies areas where further learning is required); and Intelligent Tutoring.

Intelligent Tutoring is the most sophisticated personalised learning methodology but is still in relatively early stages of development. Where it has been used effectively, the results have been extremely positive. Carnegie Learning Corporation reported that students taking their Algebra I Tutor performed 85% better than the norm on assessments of complex problem-solving skills.[i]

The potential of Intelligent Tutoring Systems lies in the fact that it combines the experience of a senior tutor with the most effective learning methodologies for each student – sometimes incorporating cognitive intelligence (eg facial recognition software and conversational interaction) to understand when students are flagging, struggling or bored.

One concern relating to personalised learning is that it reduces interaction with other students. However, by monitoring the performance of each student constantly, teachers can bring students together: either of different levels to help each other, or of similar levels to work together.

However, the major concern is whether personalised learning will create a sense of entitlement and a refusal to undertake work that students (and later employees) don't want to do?

There is a thin line between persuading students to take ownership of their studies and ensuring that learning covers all the core skills that they will need in later life.

However, if designed properly, personalised learning could prove the solution rather than the hindrance to this. By providing continual assessment and feedback, coursework can be oriented to each student (in terms of method, speed and level), which will improve understanding and therefore student engagement.

Huge sums have been invested into personalised learning systems. The Gates Foundation has invested $5 billion over the past decade on learning initiatives, with nearly $175 million going toward personalised learning development.[ii] However, it should not be seen as a replacement for teachers.

Personalised learning systems will help students learn, make them more engaged and encourage students to take more ownership of their own learning. The systems will really excel when they are embraced by an experienced teacher who can spend more time with each student building on the skills that they have learnt – in fact, changing the role of the teacher to that of a mentor or coach.

Teaching Emotional Intelligence

Project-based work and personalised learning will improve enthusiasm and effective learning, but more is needed to prepare children for the future of work. There are many ways to address this, but one addition to the armoury is to teach Social and Emotional Intelligence. When reviewing the list of attributes that make up Social and Emotional Intelligence, it is noticeable how each is required and used both in the lives of those at school and in our day-to-day lives at work.[iii] They include: self-awareness, self-management (including setting and monitoring personal and academic goals), social awareness, relationship management and responsible decision making.

The Yale Center for Emotional Intelligence has devised a programme called RULER to train teachers how to teach Emotional Intelligence. RULER (as with other Social and Emotional Intelligence programs) has resulted in better academic performance and improved Emotional Intelligence and social skills, whilst reducing anxiety and depression. Students have also gained better leadership skills. Interestingly, teaching these skills seems also to have improved the work of teachers, who have reported better relationships with students, less burnout, better relationships with the administration departments and a more positive attitude towards teaching.

If children and employees were to acquire the skills that form the basis of of WEIRD, including Emotional Intelligence, they would be well placed to face the future of work. In order for organisations to embrace these characteristics, they would need to create an environment which encourages that change. To do this, it is necessary to look at the theory of WEIRD.

Chapter 6

THE THEORY OF WEIRD

"We need to walk into the future, no matter how unnerving, with open eyes if society is to keep pace with technology."
Lawrence M. Krauss – Theoretical Physicist and Cosmologist

A) CHANGE STARTS AT THE TOP

"People buy into the leader before they buy into the vision."
John C. Maxwell – Author

One of the main qualities that we look for in our recruitment process at Pod Group is a tendency to assume that nobody else will do something as well as you. Our employees are therefore unwilling to delegate or go home until they (alone) have completed their tasks.

Having found these people, we then focus on de-programming this trait.

While this sounds at best contrary, at worst downright stupid, it works because we try to build an environment where colleagues trust each other to do the right thing - not because a process is directing what the right thing is; on the contrary, each individual has the flexibility to get things done by adjusting the process as required.

If colleagues trust each other, they are willing to accept that they may not be the best person to do everything, although this is a hard change for most people to make.

An organisation can only embrace change effectively if the CEO is 100% behind the change, understanding the need to let go of control and trust others to do their best.

Recently, one of our commercial partners wanted more details on some of the costs of our solution. We have an open book policy with partners, so I asked one of my colleagues to send over the details. Due to the way that she had presented the information, this raised some questions and concerns due to different cultural attitudes. Her reaction was: "This is an important partner, it would be better if I send the information to you first to check." Or, put another way, "Why don't you take the responsibility for this?" In the short term this would be a less risky approach, but as I explained: "We all make mistakes (especially cultural mistakes); you learnt from this and if you make another mistake we will handle it; but if I can't trust you with your work, is this your problem or mine?" On the surface she preferred to delegate the responsibility to me, but if I took that client over, in the longer term this would create a downward spiral whereby she would lose motivation and confidence as a result of not being responsible for her work. The reverse would also be true – I would feel more important and valued as I am taking more responsibility (as well as adding more tasks to my workload and therefore more stress).

There is a tendency for people to assume that, as individuals, they are vital to the organisation – and the higher you go up the organisation, the stronger that assumption becomes.

My mentor was CEO and Chairman of a public company in the US. In this position, everybody wanted a minute of his time. Within three months of his retirement, 90% of his employees, fellow managers and board members, had no time to spend with him. To be fair, it didn't bother him as he understood that he was not irreplaceable.

CEOs (and I have done this previously) have a tendency to create an environment where their role appears to be central to the day to day running of the company. They ensure that the number of decisions that they need to approve is just a little bit more than can be done efficiently. It creates a very satisfying sense of importance. This is not only done by CEOs, but by every level of management.

Then a reality check happens - often in the form of either a heart attack or a divorce. This typically leads to a reassessment of priorities. At this point, three options exist – brave (quit), stupid (carry on as before) or difficult (change how you approach life and work).

The third option is obviously the hardest, but at the end of the day the best for everybody (including family and colleagues). It requires the strength to understand that CEOs and managers don't have to take all the responsibility, and actually people prefer to shoulder their own responsibility if it means that they are in control of their own destiny. If you take the responsibility for somebody else's work – you are also taking control of a part of them and removing part of their reason for being.

If a boss is not willing to delegate responsibility, it is not possible for others to implement change further down the organisation. This is why change has to start at the top. But what to change?

B) FOCUSING ON THE THINGS THAT YOU CAN CHANGE

"The only thing that can grow is the thing you give energy to."
Ralph Waldo Emerson – Essayist

Changing attitudes is hard. It is achieved more easily when things are going badly than when they are going well.

However, it is very inadvisable to let a company reach rock bottom before introducing change as many of the key staff will already have left. Therefore, change is more effective when things are going well, to ensure that this continues. That said, it is difficult to persuade people to make changes when they are comfortable within their environment. This lack of desire to change was one of the key factors that hampered our move to WEIRD. I will explain in more detail the difficulties that we faced in the next chapter.

Rather than focusing on trying to change attitudes, it is easier to focus on taking steps that result in a change of attitudes.

In his excellent book *Reinventing Organisations*, Frederic Laloux sets out a number of organisations where the CEO has found a working compromise between typically corporate organisations (he described these as red organisations with strict command structures) and those that could be perceived as green organisations (with egalitarian management). Laloux describes these as 'Teal' organisations, the key attribute of which is that the CEO allows employees to take responsibility for their own (and therefore the company's) destiny. We have taken some of the practices used by companies cited in his book and adjusted them to our own environment.

A number of the practices that we have undertaken to help push WEIRD attitudes are discussed within the next few sections.

C) IN AND OUT

"Recently, I was asked if I was going to fire an employee who made a mistake that cost the company $600,000. No, I replied, I just spent $600,000 training him."
Thomas John Watson Sr – Ex Chairman & CEO IBM

Recruitment

I'm always baffled why companies recruit on the basis of a one-hour interview process. You wouldn't propose to marry somebody after knowing them for one hour. Granted, you are unlikely to spend the rest of your life with a new employee, but you are certainly going to spend a lot of time with them – every working day – very possibly for some years.

When I mentioned at a meeting that candidates who wish to work in our Spanish office have upwards of ten interviews, I was asked: "How can you expect people to find the time to do that?" "That's ridiculous – who would want to do that?" "It's selfish to ask!"

Although it fell on deaf ears, I tried to explain that there are three reasons for such an extensive process:

1) We try to get as many existing employees as possible to meet with the candidate. That way our employees get a say in who joins – and therefore some ownership of the recruitment decision. If an existing employee feels that they were part of the decision, they are more likely to help ensure the success of the appointment.

2) We are keen that the candidate gets an opportunity to meet the people with whom they will be working. Frankly, if somebody doesn't want to take the time to do that, it implies either that they don't care about what they do in their working day or they have doubts about how long they will be working with us.

3) At the end of the recruitment process, I will have a conversation with the candidate for more than two hours. It is difficult for somebody to keep a façade for that long, after meeting many people, so we have a high degree of confidence that the person we are interviewing is indeed the person with whom we wish to work in the future.

With the benefit of hindsight, when we have made bad recruitment decisions, it has been a result of not spending enough time interviewing the candidate.

Conflict

The enemy of conflict resolution is silence.

People should be encouraged to deal with conflict by taking it head on and talking to the person with whom they are in conflict. However, this requires a level of trust and self-confidence that is not always present. As a result, it is worth having a stepped approach to deal with conflict:

1) Sort it out privately. Initiator has to make a clear request (not a judgement or demand). The other person has to respond to request with 'yes', 'no' or a counterproposal. If there is still a conflict, then…
2) Nominate a colleague as mediator. That colleague provides support aimed at finding an agreement but does not impose a judgement or resolution. If there is still a conflict, then…
3) Select a panel of relevant colleagues, agreed upon by both parties. If the parties cannot agree on the panel, then the mediator brought in at stage 2 will decide on the panel. This panel listens, and helps shape an agreement. It cannot force a decision. If there is still a conflict, then…
4) The CEO might be added to panel. Again, the CEO is not expected to provide a decision but rather to help find a resolution to the conflict.

Any conflict should, in the first instance, stay between the two parties. Neither party should enlist the support of others unilaterally. If help is needed, it should be sought via the conflict process.

Each person should take the responsibility to talk directly to any colleague who they believe is not acting or working appropriately (appropriately is obviously the opinion of each person). Almost always, the 'problem' will be sorted by a simple conversation because, often, people are not aware that they are causing an issue, annoying other people, causing costs that they had not considered, creating more work etc. This should include the most junior person being able to speak directly to the CEO if they think the CEO is doing something wrong. True success of this system can only be demonstrated when a junior person feels comfortable taking up a conflict directly with a CEO.

This happened at Pod Group, when I was too hasty in trying to hire an employee for a new project we are launching. I walked into the office and felt that I had been set upon by four of my colleagues – and became defensive as a result. After we had all calmed down, we discussed the conflict. I was (unjustifiably) angry at the time, which resulted in a feeling in others that they couldn't express their opinion honestly. Transparency is great, but Emotional Intelligence should be used as well – if somebody feels attacked it will not lead to a useful conversation. The situation was handled much more effectively after I had calmed down and suggested that one of my colleagues spoke for the others in a separate discussion (not in the middle of the office). As a result, I understood that the real frustration was a problem on another project – so I undertook to move heaven and earth to get that problem resolved.

Dismissal

Generally, I am of the belief that there are no wrong people but rather wrong jobs. Before starting down the dismissal route, it is often worth asking what tasks the employee would prefer to do and think that they would be good at. This exercise requires both the employee and the manager or Head of HR to throw all caution to the wind and not to limit the answers to what jobs are available, what tasks need to be done, what the employee thinks they could do within the organisation or even what the company does.

By removing any pre-judgements, sometimes a very exciting business opportunity can arise with a very motivated promoter.

When employees are performing badly, there is a tendency to tighten the control around their work, with the intention of getting them to perform better. This will almost certainly lead to a downward spiral of disillusionment and poorer performance. Most employees perform badly because they are not happy with their specific role.

The quickest and most successful performance turnaround in my experience happened when we gave full responsibility for a project to a colleague who was on their final warning and due to be fired within days. Previously we had tried to control their work and taken more and more responsibility away from them. Not long after, I had the pleasure of hearing their previous boss state that he needed that person for a new project.

However, there are times that an employee has lost all motivation and is probably causing a distraction to the rest of the team. A final option is to ask the employee to set a plan as to how they are going to change. This plan needs to be set by the employee not by their manager or HR Director, so that they are responsible for its implementation. At this point there is probably a 50/50 chance that the employee will rise to the challenge. If they do not, they should be dismissed from the company as soon as it is clear that they are failing, so as not to demotivate other employees further.

D) PERFORMANCE AND REWARDS

"Our praises are our wages"
William Shakespeare – English playwright

Transparency of salaries

Part and parcel of the freedom of financial information is transparency of salaries.

However, knowing what your neighbour earns is an incredibly sensitive subject. This is strange considering that, in most countries, public servants are paid according to fairly narrow pay bands which are public knowledge.

When it comes to salaries within the private sector, obfuscation seems obligatory. From a purely financial point of view, this is advantageous to companies as they can pay what an employee will accept, not necessarily their true value. So, people can be paid different amounts for the same job.

Study after study indicates that transparent salaries create a better environment as employees realise that they are paid fairly.[i,ii]

The reverse is that non-transparent salaries lead to inaccurate assumptions. When salaries are not transparent, roughly 75% of employees will assume that they are not being paid fairly, regardless of whether their salary is above, at or below the market rate.

However, most importantly, if employees are to make informed decisions, all information needs to be transparent. The cost of each employee's salary will be one of the main costs of any new project and not including this in a budget conversation prevents the true cost of a project or business unit being analysed.

The problems we encountered in introducing transparency of salaries at Pod Group are described later. However, after the decision was made – apparently similar to other companies who have implemented this change – the actual release of salary information was a complete non-event.

Deciding own salaries

Employees deciding on their own salary is one of the key tools to generate an ethos of self-responsibility (alongside decisions on holidays, place of work and working hours). However it is a tool and not an end in itself.

Buffer, who make clever social media tools, are very public with their information. This includes publishing each person's salary online. Furthermore, Buffer publishes its financial breakdown, equity formulas and pricing breakdown.

To calculate salaries, Buffer has a formula that again is open. The third version of their pay formula is as follows:

benchmark X a cost of living multiplier X a role multiplier X an experience factor.

At Pod Group we decided that we should change the way in which salaries are calculated, resulting in huge discussions as to how a formula should be created. In summary, we couldn't find a fair equation for each person in the company living in different places, with different goals and at different times in their lives. So, finally, we realised that the only way to ensure fair salaries was to let people choose their own.

When I tell outsiders that our employees choose their own salary, the first assumption is that employees ask for outrageous salaries. I estimate that our salary bill is probably about 10% above what we would be paying without transparency and self-chosen salaries.

It is easy to explain why people are so reasonable by returning to the survey summarised in the table in Chapter 1. Around 33% of recipients were motivated to go the extra mile by: camaraderie, peer motivation, encouragement and recognition.

As salaries are transparent, employees are aware that the level of positive recognition from each of their colleagues will also take into account the salary earned. If colleagues think that you are earning too much money, there is a very real danger that your interaction with them will change. As most people value peer camaraderie, they don't want to appear greedy in the eyes of their colleagues.

Apart from peer interaction, we also provide some other tools that can help assess the appropriate salary. This includes a review of comparable salaries in each city that we operate. Each month we review the financial data of the company so that individuals can see, perhaps not individually but certainly as a group, how they are contributing.

One of the key methods to help people understand how they are viewed by their peers is a 360-degree evaluation tool that we created. However, we do not link the evaluation feedback to salaries. Instead, it is used as a way of measuring improvement and a channel to receive comments from colleagues.

Other companies have similar tools, but we decided to keep ours simple.

Evaluation and appraisals

Ray Dalio implemented a unique evaluation methodology in his company, Bridgewater Associates (one of the biggest hedge funds in the US). Employees are given iPads which they can use for various tasks. One of these is a constant evaluation process so that at any point (for example in a meeting), each employee can give a score to reflect how well a colleague is doing on any one of a hundred attributes or skills. Therefore, a twenty-five-year-old analyst can give Ray Dalio a low score for clarity during a presentation and add a comment alongside.

This methodology has its detractors, but I agree with Ray Dalio that feedback should be constant and honest. This requires a level of trust and confidence in both the giver and recipient of feedback. I hope to be able to implement constant feedback at Pod Group in the future.

At present, we have a quarterly evaluation for everybody in the company (including the CEO).

We ask just three questions:

1) How much do you know about and work with each person in the company?
2) In your opinion how much value does this person bring to the company?
3) What comment do you have about that person's work?

Initially, all comments were anonymous. However, we realised that comments can easily be taken out of context and so we now encourage people to include context in their comments and to add their name so that it can lead to further discussion.

One of our developers devised an application to ensure that the survey can be filled quickly and that the results are calculated automatically without human interaction. Most importantly of all, comments can be viewed only by the recipient and the HR Director.

In assessing the survey results, we try not to get to hung up on scores. The value is in the comments and the ability to monitor progress of individuals between evaluations.

Each person reacts to comments in very different ways – which, in itself, can lead to conflict and hurt. As a result, the HR Director talks to the recipient about any comments that might be taken badly. Hopefully, the number of problematic comments will reduce, and/or recipients will become more comfortable with constructive criticism.

E) TEAM WORKING

"Coming together is a beginning. Keeping together is progress. Working together is success."
Henry Ford – Founder of Ford Motor Company

Seating plans

The tendency in most companies is to seat departments together. There is a lot of sense to this as inter-departmental communication is facilitated.

Another option is to hot desk. Again, nothing wrong with this as it may cause more interaction between departments. Generally, though people prefer to sit together with those that they know and like.

I find that most (but not all) people prefer routine. Part of that routine is often to sit in the same place. Thus, trying to get people to change desk can create an extraordinary amount of resistance: "But we need to be with our team mates or we will have to get up and find them every time we have a question." There is logic and truth in this, but there is also value of physically splitting up a team so that they communicate with other teams.

One idea is to put the management team in desks next to each other and to put the rest of their department elsewhere. This offers two benefits:

1) Removing the manager from the team removes the ability for employees to defer even simple questions to the manager rather than thinking them through for themselves.
2) If employees come to talk to their manager, other managers get an opportunity to learn about the other departments' interactions and issues.

Similar to introducing transparent salaries, it may be worth the time and effort to persuade people that changing seats is worthwhile in order to change attitudes (especially in more hierarchical organisations). However, whilst it seems a trivial issue, forcing people to sit next to somebody against their wish can demotivate an employee such that they become disruptive. Either way, an effective seating plan can aid communication in an organisation as much as any other initiative – but finding the right time to push a change in seating is key.

Avoiding stars and egos

For WEIRD to work successfully, trust is required and this arises when people are honest with themselves and with others – knowing their strengths and willing to admit their weaknesses.

There are of course many team-building exercises which can be very valuable in developing trust between colleagues. However, most important is the day-to-day encouragement of trust.

Teams will always outperform individual stars when each person understands and appreciates that they need their colleagues in order to achieve their own and the company's goals.

This requires only two actions:

1) Refuse to pander to a 'star's' ego. Even though they may be responsible for much of the company's revenue, in the long term they will destroy the company as other people won't want to work with them. Furthermore, the longer they stay, the more dependent upon their 'star' status the company will become.
2) Make sure that anybody with an over-inflated ego understands what everybody else in the organisation does. People generally think they are the most important because they don't understand the value of other people's work.

Worse than an over-inflated ego is pride. Some years ago, in another company, I was pulled into a bitter multi-million-dollar dispute by two investors. Each was very proud and refused to back down. The result: both lost all their money and their reputations – but the lawyers did well. Creating an environment where people can admit they are wrong or admit their lack of knowledge without fearing repercussions is extremely healthy. The easiest way to start and encourage this environment is for the CEO to take a lead in publicly accepting what he or she doesn't know and to apologise publicly when making a mistake.

A CEO offering a sincere apology directly to a customer can often breed better customer loyalty than any other action. A sincere apology offered to an employee when the CEO has made a mistake will mend more bridges than any other action.

Organisation and Teams

People often mix the WEIRD philosophy with Holacracy. WEIRD is not Holacracy. In fact, it is almost the opposite.

Holacracy creates circles of self-organising teams using a very detailed framework of how these circles should interact with each other. Goals and purposes are set by higher circles which are then passed down to lower circles. There is much emphasis on the administrative procedures to be used internally, with little emphasis on external – ie customer – interaction. Each circle of holacracy involves weighty democratic procedures.

WEIRD on the other hand is not a democratic process. People are encouraged to take and be responsible for their decisions after seeking advice. It emphasises the need for employees to be able to make, and take responsibility for, decisions that will have a direct financial impact on the company.

However, whilst individual decision-making is vital, people still need to work within teams.

Any change process can only work effectively if people are willing to accept it. About a year before we started our change to WEIRD, I tried to re-focus the company organisational structure around projects and products rather than departments. I failed, as nobody was interested and didn't see the need. So, I put it on the back burner and kept it in mind.

A year later we started our change to WEIRD; people understood the need for change and though it was difficult, that change has been successful. However, I decided to keep the departmental structure unchanged so as not to have too many moving parts at once.

So WEIRD 1.0 was based on retaining department (or project) heads, using their experience to act as a coach to team members, rather than a manager.

Their role is to act as a point of contact for that department, ensuring that all the parts are heading in the same direction and that these relate to what else is happening in the company. They also take the lead on strategic thinking and ensure that cross-communication between departments stays on track.

A year on, people are beginning to see the disadvantage of departments which create silos of 'them' and 'us' and encourage blame – "We couldn't sell more as 'Development' didn't deliver on time and 'Support' screwed up with a major lead." Development and Support in this case are not individuals and therefore easy to blame without getting personal. More importantly, communication does not flow effectively because department heads are left with the sole responsibility to communicate. Finally, budgeting is calculated on how much each department needs to do its job for the year rather than relating this to profit.

We have now progressed to WEIRD 2.0 – the move from departments to teams. People move into and out of teams depending upon the product (we have internally split our products by type of customer) or by project. Joining a team is voluntary, but if a team member's input is required at all in that project, it is expected that they will be in that team. Some team members may play a very minor role, whilst others could be working within that team full time. Some people may be in ten teams, others only in one. The team is not managed by any one individual, but coordinated by someone who may or may not be the most senior person in terms of experience

If the objectives of the team start to get muddled, the team will split itself up further so that the role of each group is clear. We have about thirty projects or products running at any one time. Some will involve one or two people; most include about eight and occasionally (for the implementation of WEIRD) they will include everybody (split into more manageable sub-groups).

Any person can suggest and take the lead in forming a new team, and each team has its own budget and its own profit and loss account. When a new team is formed which requires budget, the coordinator of that team will confer with other team coordinators as to what monies can be moved into a central pot for new products or projects. This ensures that budgets don't stay allocated when they could be better used elsewhere.

The best part about splitting the company into teams is that, as most teams will include people from different departments or geographical regions, employees are forced to talk to those outside their own department which improves company communication.

F) OWNERSHIP AND RESPONSIBILITY

"You cannot escape the responsibility of tomorrow by evading it today."
Abraham Lincoln – Former US President

Transparency of company financial information

There is a tendency amongst most CEOs and managers to hoard information – especially financial information. Information is power after all. However, the excuses given for not providing financial information to employees are never about power but:

- "It's confidential, competitors might get hold of it."
- "We don't want to worry employees."
- "Only senior management need it as only they make the decisions based on the financial results."
- "We've always kept our financial information confidential – why would we change?"

Let me debunk these in quick succession.

- If a CEO can't trust their employees not to give financial information to competitors, then why are these employees working for the company?
- Employees (in fact everybody) will always assume the worst based on gossip and Chinese whispers. By 'not worrying' employees, they will almost certainly cause more anxiety. Furthermore, not worrying employees is at best paternalistic, at worst condescending. If employees can be trusted to work within the company, there is no reason why they shouldn't be trusted with financial information.
- Decisions are made all the way down the chain – every day. Why do only senior managers get to make decisions based on all the facts? Without the financial information, it is impossible for others to make informed decisions.

- Let's turn the last question around. Why wouldn't a CEO wish employees to see the financial details of the company (apart from the feeling of power)?

An answer to the last question could be that if CEOs are able to take decisions on the basis of information available only to them, nobody else can question that decision. If all information is available to everybody, then anybody is qualified to question any decisions made in the organisation – including those made by the CEO. Some CEOs think that they need to be right at all times, but they will gain far more respect by admitting they are wrong or by asking advice from those who can help them make a better decision.

Making financial information available to all employees is always easier in the end. The truth may be unpleasant at the time, but most people can handle the truth – it's lies they struggle with. Likewise, most people can handle a bit of bad financial news if they feel that they know what is going on. What is far harder to handle is sudden financial shocks which will affect somebody's job and possibly their livelihood.

Therefore, the power of sharing all information should not be underestimated.

However, sharing the information does not necessarily lead to employees being interested in it. Employees will not usually search for the company's financial information unless persuaded to do so. We have tried to break down the information into easier key performance indicators that we review each month, but still I am concerned that so few people actually know or care about the financial situation of the company. One way of addressing this has been to create and impart financial information that is useful and relevant to each team.

Company policies (eg holidays, expenses, flexi-hours, training)

As mentioned earlier, at Pod Group we avoid company policies where possible. Here, I will provide a little more description on how we achieve that:

a) Holidays

We keep no record of when people take holidays. If somebody is taking holiday, they update the shared calendar. Checking this calendar is normally the second action after asking, "Anybody know if David is in today?"

The only thing that we ask is that if people are going on holiday, even if it is a last-minute decision, they make sure that they are not going to leave their colleagues having to do more work as a result of their absence.

Our holiday policy did initially cause a problem. When we started, we needed to encourage people to take holidays. Is this still the case? I'm not sure as we don't keep records, but I certainly feel the need to remind people to take more holidays.

b) Expenses

We don't check expenses. We don't approve expenses. There is no point giving a daily expense allowance – some days a sandwich is sufficient, other days a three-course lunch. This will depend on location, mood, client meetings – in fact too many factors to account for.

So, we tell people to spend their money as they would normally. Then claim it back. Employees should be trusted with expenses in the same way as any other decision they make for the company.

c) Flexi-hours

I still haven't worked out the best time to come into the office if I want to find people. Some people are definitely morning people and others you wouldn't want to see before they've had at least two coffees. Thankfully those people generally don't arrive until they have had their two cups of coffee – which could be around 11 am.

By letting people find their own rhythm, we find that people work better – forcing people to be working by a certain time or working within specific hours doesn't take account of other circumstances in each person's life. As a parent, I know the value of being able to take my children to school. For others it might be incredibly important to wake up slowly, or to go to the gym when it is quiet.

d) Place of work

The ex-Yahoo CEO, Marissa Mayer, much to the annoyance of many staff, insisted that all employees return to working in the office when many were used to working at home.

As with all things, I firmly believe flexibility is required, but sometimes having people in the same place can improve communication exponentially compared to remote working. There are a number of very successful companies where all staff work remotely, so clearly it can work, but our experience is that more can be achieved in an hour's face to face meeting than a morning of video calling.

That said, it is more important to encompass flexibility with regard to place of work. When doing tasks that do not require communication with others, I will generally work at home. One of our CEOs lives in a remote location – working from home is his only option. One of our operations staff spends January in her home country every year. We have a reasonable number of employees who will combine a couple of weeks' holiday with a month working in their home country.

As with all things WEIRD, if you let people decide for themselves, they will find the solution that is best for them and the company.

e) Training

In theory, undertaking training in order to learn and develop skills is a must in any organisation. However, training can add stress as the day job still needs to be completed. Our training policy is rather like our holiday policy – do as much as you like; we'll pay for it.

Sending people on obligatory training courses is a sure-fire way to breed resentment. Some people do not want to go, and as a result they will not concentrate or learn. The time and money will be wasted and then they feel more stress from having to catch up on their work.

If, however, you leave people to choose the most appropriate training courses, maybe with some advice (which they are free to ignore) from HR, they will be motivated to learn and will manage their own work much better.

If people feel responsible for their work, they are loath to spend time doing something that may not have a direct impact on productivity. Some people love to be taught, others prefer to learn on the job. Either way, it is always beneficial for people to decide for themselves what and how to learn, even if it isn't directly related to the employee's work. If the company pays for it and allows the time off to do it, it will be viewed as one of the best company benefits they receive.

Recently, Udemy offered all of their courses for a ridiculously low price and collectively we signed up for about twenty courses. Will all of the information learned be utilised? I don't know, but it was fascinating to see what interested people as well as how they often chose courses which, while (mostly) related to the company, were certainly outside the sphere of their present role.

Expensive courses with little perceived value can cause as much tension as a perceived over-inflated salary. Therefore, peer pressure will ensure training value for money.

Roles vs tasks

People like roles. It gives a sense of value and security. "This is my role, I am an expert and I can do things related to this role."

However, within a role exist tasks and by focusing more on these, it is possible to get people to expand the role to fit the tasks instead of restricting themselves to those tasks that fit a role.

Roles fit within departments, reinforcing an attitude of "we are the best people to undertake any tasks related to this role". As roles are easily defined within a job, people naturally want to defend a role so as to protect their job security. If other people could undertake parts of the role, it may make the job redundant. This leads to a hoarding of information to hinder the ability of others to do part of the role. This is one reason that companies have communication problems.

In a hierarchical organisation, although employees can be responsible for a task, their manager is normally responsible for the role and employees are uncomfortable working on tasks outside that role because the lines of communication and responsibility are unclear.

Focusing on tasks rather than roles therefore avoids many problems.

Often a task (or a series of tasks that make a project) will fall across different departments. Making employees responsible for a task removes the need for departmental management and encourages employees to work with people from other departments.

So how is this implemented in practice? The first and simplest step is to change each employee's role into a list of tasks with a catch-all at the end, eg '...and any other tasks that the employee wishes to undertake that would benefit the company'. However, to reduce resistance on the part of employees when removing the security of a role, they must be the ones to define and agree the tasks.

Next, employees should be encouraged to get involved in tasks that lie outside their department; and when starting a new task or project, they should be encouraged to consider whether somebody from another department could add experience or a different perspective.

Similarly to the advice process, pushing tasks across the company may slow the work down initially, but this is easily outweighed by the speed of subsequent integration, improved communication and the success of the completed task.

Eventually, people will stop thinking of their roles in terms of department roles, but rather as a series of tasks that make a role that has an influence on many parts of the company.

Decisions

The decision-making process is the hardest part of WEIRD.

Within Pod Group, each person in the company can make any decision, including an investment decision. There is a caveat to this – the decision must not put the company at risk. Those making decisions must first seek advice from appropriate people. As every person in the company has access to all the financial information, the decision-making process undertaken by that individual should include the financial implications of that decision. A CEO should not overrule a decision, as this would undermine the WEIRD approach.

That is the theory. The practice is harder.

Generally, when somebody wants to make a decision that will involve money, they will talk to the financial manager who needs to understand that they are not expected to give an opinion; otherwise all decisions related to spending will depend upon whether or not the financial manager thinks it's a good idea. Therefore, the role of the financial manager is to request money from the CFO or the CEO to support a decision made by somebody else in the company.

The advice process involves not only receiving (hopefully) good suggestions, but more importantly bringing others into the decision-making process. It is necessary to seek the advice of those you think will be against your decision. Talking through the positives and negatives with them makes it clear that their objections have been taken on board. Having done this, it is very likely that rather than objecting, that person will now be an advocate for the idea. If other people see that the main objector is now a supporter, others will probably back the idea as well.

I can look back at all the decisions that I made prior to starting the WEIRD process and tell which of those decisions I made alone. Regardless of the profitability or practicality of these decisions, none were fully supported by my colleagues – and thus did not achieve their potential. During the writing of this book, a couple of times I tried to push a decision faster than my colleagues were willing to accept it, and each time I backed off as I realised that it would be a failure without internal support.

This is not a process of decision by consensus – which generally results in weak decisions because the original idea is watered down to please everybody. After taking advice, the decision needs to be made and owned. If it turns out to be a bad decision, this is not the responsibility of those who provided advice – but of the decision maker.

However, a manager or CEO should always applaud a decision made – regardless of outcome. For an organisation to progress, employees should be encouraged to make decisions without fear of blame.

The hard part of WEIRD decision-making is for managers and the CEO to refrain from taking control. People will always defer to somebody perceived to have power over them. Therefore, a manager or CEO needs to ensure that:

- They always ask everybody else for their opinions without giving their own.
- They keep a poker face.
- They express no opinion, but ask questions that lead the person to reach their own decision.

- They always leave with a "well you decide" or "so you decided that".

Managers and CEOs are used to telling people what to do and employees expect their superior to make the decision. Giving employees ownership and responsibility is a reversal of this custom.

Despite this, managers and CEOs usually have more experience and can often predict which decisions are likely to be disastrous. It is necessary for them to decide whether this could be a learning experience or dangerous for the employee and the company. If they feel it will be a learning experience without any long-term damage, then it is better to let the employee make the mistake. However, if the decision could damage the company then it is worth leading the decision maker to a different conclusion by asking some searching questions.

Strategy

There are two ways to decide and implement strategy. From the top down or the bottom up.

Top down strategies carry the same risk as that set out earlier in the description of dictators – the success of the company is reliant on the quality of the CEO. Also, they will not necessarily get support from those who are tasked to implement them.

One alternative is the traditional bottom-up approach, where employees suggest strategies that are then sent up the ladder for the CEO to decide. This has the advantage of getting input from those at the ground level as well as a diversity of ideas but can lead to disappointment and lack of support if the decision from 'on-high' does not take account of some of the ideas passed up the chain.

As part of our WEIRD process we are implementing a strategic process to start at the bottom – and stay close to the bottom.

Our first step was to set out the corporate strategy. Previously we had vision statements and company goals – but as these were created by myself and a few managers, it is unlikely that anyone else in the company could tell you what they were. So, we changed it to two simple company goals:

'Enjoy ourselves' and 'Make money' (in that order).

A few of us discussed creating a more comprehensive and focused corporate goal, but it became clear that in so doing we would set limits on each individual's goals.

We ask each individual to set out a strategy as to how they can contribute to the units within which they have joined. Each team then joins those individual strategies to others, creating a strategy for each unit. This is assisted by listing the skills and goals of each unit member. The unit then reviews these and decides what can and can't be achieved and where goals coincide. From this, the goal of the unit is established and projections and budgets calculated.

The goal is then shared with other units, and written feedback can be given by any other individual or unit wishing to make suggestions, offer their services or point out where units can coordinate activities.

Thus there is no need for a company-wide strategy. In fact, by not pushing the strategic decisions up the chain, it is apparent that the buck stops at unit level. If a unit is doing something that is detrimental to another unit, first it is likely that some individuals will be on both units and will point this out at an early stage; and secondly, by communicating directly, units will find a better solution than one imposed from above.

And the financial goals of the company as a whole? These are made up from the sum of the parts. There is no point in management making a multi-million-dollar arbitrary target when a far more realistic estimation can be made by those who have to implement it.

As to the strategic goals of the company, likewise trust needs to be given to the units so that they will coordinate sufficiently to build a sensible overall strategy. There may be no stated overall company goal but the conglomerate of unit goals will be flexible enough to change, direct enough to implement and probably more profitable than any strategy imposed from above.

If it is clear that a strategic goal of the company is missing – this is easy to resolve by creating another unit to fill the hole. Employees and managers do not have to be re-oriented, budgets do not need to be re-done and new strategic goals do not need to be communicated.

American football coach, Paul Bryant, explained the advantage of keeping strategy at a team, rather than company level: "A good, quick, small team can beat a big, slow team any time."

Ownership of the business

It will come as no surprise that one way to encourage employees to feel responsibility and ownership of their work is to make them owners of the business.

Whether this takes the form of stock options, shares, cooperative shares, partnership or any other form of ownership doesn't really matter. It is preferable if the employees (or a designated committee of employees) choose the structure of ownership or at least have the power to change the structure if they see fit. The CEO, CFO and any other major shareholders should not decide how that structure is formulated, otherwise employees may feel that they have been manipulated.

A fair rule of thumb to provide genuine ownership is to provide 25% of shares for employees.

Prior to shares being traded publicly, owning shares in a company when there is little or no market to trade them makes it difficult for employees to see their value. If the company has a clear goal to undertake an IPO at some set point, they automatically take on a higher perceived value. Otherwise, the value of the shares will only be realised if and when the company gets acquired.

Until this point, the quantifiable value of those shares rests in paid dividends. However, paying dividends when the company is focused on growing is counter-intuitive as profits should be invested in further growth. Paying a small dividend provides an unexpected bonus for employees at the end of the year. With transparency, the employees will understand that they are being rewarded to the detriment of profits being ploughed back to fuel growth. Better still, ask the employees to choose whether to pay a dividend or not – after all, they are part owners of the company.

One thing that always bemuses me is companies that give share options to employees that can be retained after the employee leaves the company. Why would you want an ex-employee to hold shares? Shares should be owned by those with an active interest in the company, not those that are moving elsewhere. As a result, when an employee leaves our company they no longer own shares or have options in the company. In some cases, this is linked to a pay-out formula, but in most it is not.

The tools that I have mentioned above help put people in the right frame of mind to follow WEIRD practices. It is worth reinforcing again – these tools are not goals in themselves, but rather a structure in which WEIRD can flourish. I have added a summary of them below:

Table 6.1 Summary of WEIRD practices

WEIRD Practice	Summary
In and Out	
Recruitment Process	Take enough time to get to know any candidate and let them know the company. Check skills but concentrate on getting to know their attitude and what is important for them.
Conflict	Any conflict needs to be resolved by those affected through a conflict process.

Dismissal	Is the person in the wrong role? Poor performance arises from a bored employee. Removing responsibility will create worse performance, so increase responsibility before any dismissal.
Performance and Rewards	
Transparency of Salaries	Required for all employees to make investment decisions as salaries account for a major part of costs. Transparent salaries remove conflict and gender discrepancy.
Deciding Own Salaries	Salary formulae will always work for some, not others. Allowing people to choose salaries will remove a demotivator. Peer pressure should ensure salaries do not get excessive.
Evaluation and Appraisals	Honest feedback is required for people to improve. Regular evaluations for everybody are part of this.
Team Working	
Seating Plans	People like routine and who they sit next to but getting people to mix brings great communication benefits.
Avoiding Stars and Egos	Teams are far more productive than stars. Get rid of stars who don't want to be part of the team.
Organisation and Teams	If possible remove departments and focus on teams based around projects and products. Allow people to join and leave teams according to the value they feel they can add.
Ownership and Responsibility	
Transparency of Company Financial Information	Employees have to understand all of the financials of the company to make even the smallest decision. People don't need to be shielded from information. The more information employees possess, the more informed the decision.
Company Policies (Holidays, Expenses,	No company policies are required. Trust employees to be reasonable and not leave

Flexi-hours, Place of Work, Training)	their colleagues in trouble. Employees can better decide where to work, training etc. than managers.
Roles vs Tasks	Aim to focus on tasks, not roles. People get stuck in roles, whereas tasks come and go.
Decisions	Allow and encourage employees to make decisions by getting advice from colleagues.
Strategy	Let the strategy flow from bottom-up, not top-down.
Ownership of the Business	Giving shares to all employees breeds ownership. Ownership is the strongest motivator.

Setting up WEIRD practices is a hard job to start. It is even more difficult to keep people following these practices.

G) CHANGE, REINFORCEMENT AND GETTING EVERYBODY ON BOARD

"A leader is best when people barely know he exists; when his work is done, his aim fulfilled, they will say: we did it ourselves."
Lao Tzu – Ancient Chinese Philosopher

The ironic thing about trying to get each person in a company to take responsibility for themselves is that sometimes the CEO needs to be an autocrat to make this happen.

I have also mentioned that implementing WEIRD requires the CEO to be fully behind the idea of letting go of control.

The problem is to marry these two concepts. The CEO needs to know when to be autocratic and when to relinquish control.

Implementing WEIRD requires a CEO and managers to exercise a high level of Emotional Intelligence and understand how each employee is likely to perceive a comment. Some employees will embrace self-management more than others – they will be more likely to accept a suggestion as advice that can be ignored. Somebody who is less confident will perceive the same suggestion as an order.

Therefore, learning the art of staying silent (especially around less confident colleagues) is a key skill.

Changing a traditional organisation to one of self-management cannot be achieved by words alone. From our experience, the tools above help employees and managers to start to think differently.

However, it is important not to swap one system of control with another. When a colleague says, "We haven't done it the WEIRD way" I still need to explain that there is no single 'way' but rather an openness in mentality which people can use to achieve their goals.

That said, people do like structure. If you removed all structure and told people to be responsible for themselves, they wouldn't know what this meant or how to do it. This is the difficulty in practising WEIRD. The company needs enough structure to provide security whilst ensuring that there is enough flexibility to allow those who can to soar. There is no simple or prescriptive answer. As always when trying to make a change, it is worth finding a few disciples and build from there. Timing is also key. There are times when changes can be pushed through and times when people need to be allowed to adjust.

There is no right and wrong way to implement self-management or WEIRD. The next two chapters of this book include some weekly blog posts that I wrote in the first six months of Pod Group's change to WEIRD. This is *a* – but not *the* – way to do it. Not least because we made a lot of mistakes (which I will highlight), but most of all because a company is made up of individuals – and any change needs to be oriented to those individuals.

There is no moment that a company can say it has succeeded in implementing WEIRD (or any other methodology of self-management). However, it is well on course when employees organise their own company-wide meeting and decide how investment decisions should be circulated and reviewed. This is also the moment at which, as a company owner, you realise that you no longer own the company. As a CEO you realise that you are now co-CEO, with all of your colleagues and you will accept decisions that you would not have made.

H) WOMEN AND WEIRD

"Whatever women do they must do twice as well as men to be thought half as good. Luckily, this is not difficult."
Charlotte Whitton – Ex-Mayor of Ottawa, Canada

One of the side effects of WEIRD is that it overcomes some of the disadvantages experienced by women at work.

A study on Emotional Intelligence by the Korn Ferry Hay Group analysed data from 55,000 professionals from 90 countries. In 11 out of 12 Emotional Intelligence competencies, women showed greater levels of Emotional Intelligence than men (in the 12th, women and men were the same).[iii]

Teams work best when the team members display higher levels of Emotional Intelligence. As females are shown to have higher levels of Emotional Intelligence than males, we actively seek female colleagues and, despite being in a male dominated industry, we keep a fairly good 50/50 ratio.

One of the tools we implemented to encourage self-responsibility was transparency of pay. This has an intended side effect – equalisation of gender salaries. In our main office, women earn on average about 15% more than men mainly because many of our female employees are in more senior positions than the men.

So why does the gender pay gap still exist in many companies? Generally, we have seen that, at the interview stage, if a man is asked whether he can do something – the answer is almost always a resounding yes (despite no forethought or experience). When a woman is asked the same, she will look back at her experience and reflect on whether she has done something similar before. Men sell themselves harder at the interview stage, which includes demanding more money. Most companies are trying to get the most value for the least money, so if a woman asks for less than a man (or less commonly, vice versa) – the company doesn't object.

This is a false economy because, at some point, the woman will find out that she is paid less than a male colleague for the same job. At this point motivation is lost, a bitter environment created and eventually the team's performance will fall.

With transparency of salaries, if women are paid less they are armed with the information to demand equal pay. If the company does not provide this then, at best, trust in the organisation will be eroded. At worst the company is opening itself to potential legal action.

One of my female colleagues recently wrote a blog on how we need to increase the proportion of women in technical jobs. Perhaps she should be careful as to what she wishes for. The jobs that are more likely to be lost to Artificial Intelligence are those which are more process driven with less requirement for Emotional Intelligence, ie jobs predominantly held by men.

This chapter has provided an overview of how it is possible to implement WEIRD practices, but the reality can be very different. The next chapter covers the change to WEIRD within Pod Group. It wasn't always easy but, drawing on blogs that were written at the time, I aim to present a realistic picture of the pitfalls and successes that we went through during our change process.

Chapter 7

DESTROYING THE OLD POD WORLD

"To destroy is always the first step in any creation."
E. E. Cummings

THE COMPANY – POD GROUP

I started PodSystem (now called Pod Group) in 1999. I patented and sold a box for engineers to receive parts at a remote location on the way to their next job (think lockers for suitcases in railway stations). The next ten years were not successful – creating and selling various hardware and software solutions related to what is now IoT, whilst providing SIM cards to partners. Realising that I needed to change, I decided to focus on providing SIM cards for IoT devices around the world. Since then Pod Group has grown to approximately fifty people and is moving towards a turnover of $10 million per annum with six offices (and counting) on four continents.

In the last section, I set out the characteristics of WEIRD – Wisdom, Emotional Intelligence, Initiative, Responsibility and (Self) Development. In theory, implementation should be easy. The reality is that you cannot just tell people to use wisdom or take responsibility for their work. To persuade people to use WEIRD attributes, it is necessary to create an environment that encourages WEIRD behaviour.

At Pod Group, we tried to involve all our staff in the change to WEIRD. The first part of the change process (now referred to as WEIRD 1.0) was gaining acceptance that the prevailing structure wasn't sustainable and needed changing – whilst still keeping things running.

The first six months were the hardest, and the blogs below were written during that time. These are absolutely not intended to show how WEIRD should be implemented; but are a record of how we decided to implement change considering the individuals involved. The present tense used in this section refers to the time that I wrote the blog.

MONEY IS A NON-MOTIVATOR – (WEEK 2)

Money is a non-motivator. It took me only 47 years to realise this.

When employing staff, I thought that if we offered unlimited bonuses as a percentage of gross profit, everybody would be happy.

Wrong.

So, what could be wrong about motivating with unlimited bonuses? At the moment, everybody receives a percentage of the gross profit above a threshold that reflects when they joined the company. Bonuses are paid after a couple of months of joining regardless of position, but percentages differ according to experience.

This week, we discovered why money is a non-motivator and I should have known better. Dan Pink has a very good TED talk on this[i], the summary of which is that money is a great incentive when tasks are narrow (eg building widgets). However, for jobs that rely on creativity (or at least handling multiple variables – which accounts for most office jobs), financial incentives have been proven in multiple studies over the last 40 years to create worse performance than where no financial incentive is provided. The reason for this is that people get too focused and don't look at factors unrelated to the incentive.

So, the philosophising (he is Greek after all) HR Director and I sat down with everybody.

We explained that, as we said and confirmed in writing when they were hired, we would need to change people's bonus thresholds and percentages to reflect a smaller part of a bigger pie. It wouldn't mean that they would receive less bonus, but that their bonus would grow at a slower rate.

Through this process I discovered that money is a non-motivator. As:

- So long as they were paid reasonably, most people want to do a good job regardless of the money.

- A few people didn't (and I think still don't) understand that the bonus was meant to be part of their overall salary. Net result – they were upset that their salary hadn't increased and thought their progress in the company wasn't being reflected properly. I was at a loss how to answer this, as the bonus had added a significant amount of money to each person's monthly take home pay.

- Despite salaries and bonuses being considerably higher than the market rate, it seemed that earning less salary than a colleague was more of an issue than the amount taken home.

- In another case, reducing the percentage above a new threshold was viewed as a negative reflection of the employee's performance. The bonus wouldn't reduce, but clearly the perceived value had.

It was at this point that I remembered why I vowed never again to run a company with more than a few employees (the last one was 150 people across 8 countries) until I found a better way of doing it. Dealing with people was too hard.

Then I thought about our holiday policy (or lack thereof). It was almost management hassle free – people did what they wanted. The reason why it is almost, rather than totally, management hassle free is that I have to push people to take holidays.

CREATING THE PERFECT ORGANISATION (OPTIMISTICALLY) – (WEEK 4)

"Did you come up with these ideas before or after you got drunk?" Slanderous accusations emerged from our colleagues when my HR Director and I returned to the office to explain our two-day disappearance.

"Did you go abroad? Was it a nice spa hotel?"

How little they knew ....

We had traversed our way into the depths of the Andalucian countryside with no heating and the nearest house at least a mile away to make sure we couldn't be disturbed.

A recurring theme of this change process is that people don't like change. Our colleagues were worried about what plans we were going to concoct in our cold isolation. Once we explained where we had been, that obviously our drinking habits were only to stay warm, what the goal of our retreat had been and they were given a broad overview of what we were thinking, everybody seemed less nervous and more curious.

Two days (and much wine) resulted in a presentation of some of the practices that we could adopt. Some of the slides have been added below. First our vision.

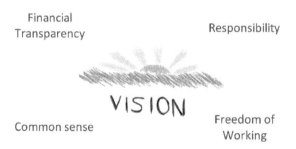

...which will result in one overall aim:

Everybody takes responsibility for their own growth and success, which will lead to the growth and success of the company.

However, there are some issues that, if not handled properly, could be disastrous. This is especially true when allowing any employee to spend company resources as they wish.

One of the hardest parts of this journey so far is the realisation that if we go down the route of transparent salaries and financial information – then, like everyone else, I need to be willing to reveal my earnings. Furthermore, with 360-degree evaluations, if they are to have any weight, I can be fired as MD and there will be a need for me to find another role:

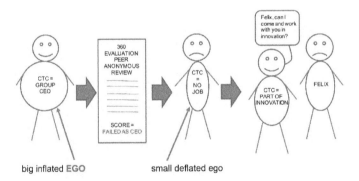

It is difficult to suggest a new way to go forward whilst avoiding any suggestions as to how it will actually work – especially when people are used to the final say coming from the CEO. So, we have to keep our suggestions more speculative for the moment, so as not to lead the conversation.

We have, however, tried to set out a number of questions to resolve, including how profit should be divided.

PRESENTING TO THE TEAM: GIVE NO ANSWERS – (WEEK 5)

"We are trying to get a bunch of control freaks to take control of their own actions – and they're afraid!" As a company, Pod Group is full of control freaks (we employ them on purpose), so being afraid of taking control wasn't a reaction we were expecting.

This week we made our presentation to the team. To do this we created groups (fairly randomly) of three or four people and set aside two hours for our presentation to each group over a two-day period.

We were careful to stress that we weren't making suggestions, but rather that we wanted people to think about how the company should be structured going forward (especially around responsibility, salaries and goals).

That said, one of the key points that we were trying to make was the concept of employees choosing their goals and the company fitting in with this rather than the other way around.

This brings up the question, "What is the purpose of a company?" For a public company, there is a fiduciary duty to shareholders, but as I am intending to put some of the shares in trust for the employees anyway – this question gets more complicated.

So, what was the reaction after the presentation?

Silence.

Followed by *"How do you cope with being you?"*

Followed by *"It's your baby; why do you want to give it up?"*

Again, not reactions we were expecting or hoping for! So, I tried to explain that as with any baby they grow and as they get bigger you can't control everything. However, more importantly, I tried to explain that if we made use of everybody's brains and initiative, we would go further than being limited by a hierarchical model where the organisation's capacity to grow is always going to be limited by the capabilities and bandwidth of the CEO. Explained in this way, it seemed obvious to my colleagues that change was required (I decided not to read anything into the ease with which everybody understood it).

But still they were afraid.

BEST IF THE BOSS LEAVES – (WEEK 6)

The ironic thing about trying to move people to self-management is that it requires autocracy to make it happen.

I was on a trip this week which provided a good opportunity for people to talk freely amongst themselves without me interfering. However, five days on, radio silence seems to be the preferred reaction.

After an email kick, we started getting responses on the forum on our intranet. As an indicator, here are some of the questions that have been posted on the forum:

- What are related podcasts, articles and books?

- How/when/who decides if we hire a new person/make an investment?

- What is common sense for making decisions?

- From the monthly gross profit, how much should the business distribute to its employees as wages (salaries+bonuses)? (Please say a %)

- Should we choose our own salaries?

- Should everybody be able to see all the expenses of the company (including salaries)?

- What about a training pot?

Whilst some people have been active on the forum, there are some who don't want to put their opinion down in writing. To try to bring these people into the conversation, I have had to encourage (from afar) people to take company time to go and talk amongst themselves and especially to take time to read around the subject.

At this point, we cannot put any timescale on when we can move forward as we need to get people used to the idea of changing to a radically different way of working.

Before I left, I was shocked when two of our technical team wanted to know how the gross profit was calculated. Both had been in the company for over a year, bonuses based on gross profit was a fundamental part of our remuneration structure and they didn't know on what basis they were being paid. I am sure there are many others who don't know how their salaries are calculated and we must find a way to ensure that people care how the company is progressing financially.

PEOPLE HATE CHANGE – (WEEK 7)

"What time are you leaving for lunch? Ah good, I'll make sure I use the kitchen then."

If nothing else, after trying to move to self-management, I will have greater self-awareness. The above question came from one of our account management team after I had said that I would work in the kitchen so that anybody could come and ask questions about the process we are going through. I am happy to report that our coffee expenditure has reduced this week and I have had much time to concentrate.

However, the occasional person forgot that I was in the kitchen so, in return for letting them get their coffee, I wanted their feedback. This has resulted in three observations to date:

1) Giving people enough time to read around the subject is vital. We are a long way from full acceptance, but the general reaction was that "I could see that maybe it could work, but I know others won't be happy". This is progress from "You're mad". What was interesting about the 'others won't be happy' is that I haven't found the 'others' yet, so I am still trying to work out whether they genuinely thought there were others for whom self-management wouldn't work – or was a reflection of their own doubts.

2) Undertaking this exercise across 5 different countries and around 10 languages definitely adds to the communication challenges.

3) People hate change.

Some of the arguments against moving to self-management have made no sense. *"Self-management can work for a company like Semco, which is a production company, but we work in an office – so it wouldn't work here."* I talked to our US CEO, who pointed out something interesting – most of the people who opposed our proposals were women.

Again, this makes no sense. One reason for the gender pay gap is said to be that women don't negotiate as hard over their level of pay as men. Transparent salaries overcome this issue as companies cannot use secrecy to get away with paying women less. So why in our company, where we have a fairly even gender mix, were women objecting?

I asked. Perhaps we have made our work environment too comfortable, but it appears that the main reason for concern was not because of what we were suggesting, but rather that people don't like change. There is no magic bullet to overcome this, apart from convincing people that the change is worth the risk.

I am thinking that a PhD in behavioural economics could be helpful in this process.

MOVING TO STAGE TWO OF THE CHANGE PROCESS – (WEEK 8)

"Is this a game?"

Once again, not a reaction I had expected (I'm beginning to cease to be amazed by the reactions that I am getting from Pod Group's move to self-management).

I refrained from the sarcastic response, *"Yes, I thought it would be fun to put the whole company in disarray, offer no solutions and see if it survives".*

"No" seemed a better answer. Followed by *"Why?"*

"I can't see what we are doing".

If you have been following these blogs, you may be spotting a recurring theme – lack of communication from the CEO (me). The trouble with trying to get people to move to self-management is exactly that – you can't dictate the whole process, otherwise it will feel like a solution dropped from above rather than agreed between colleagues. So ironically a lack of communication and lack of action is required to allow people to find their own solutions.

I realised this week, however, that a compromise is needed between those people who are keen on the concepts around self-management and those for whom these concepts were new and uncomfortable.

Without moving forward, momentum will be lost and uncertainty towards this process of change will derail what we are trying to achieve. So, it was time to get everybody moving past the reading stage.

So, I set out the steps of the process:

- Stage 1. Introduce the concepts of self-management, read around the subject and start with some initial viewpoints.

- Stage 2. Collect suggestions for concrete plans, comment and merge plans until processes have been agreed on each aspect of self-management including: salaries, responsibility, reviews, investment and dispute resolution.

- Stage 3. Collect all of the relevant internal and external information to allow the plan in stage 2 to be implemented

- Stage 4. Implementation

- Stage 5. Review and evolve

After talking to each person about their reaction to the concepts that we were trying to introduce, I needed to know whether there was anybody in the company who was uncomfortable with the whole concept and didn't want to change. So, we sent an anonymous survey focused around four subjects:

1) Transparency of all company figures and other relevant information
2) Taking on the responsibility of managing oneself. This may or may not include everybody being able to make an investment decision related to their own work.
3) Choosing your own salary and/or bonus
4) Transparency of salaries

and allowed for one of four responses to each subject;

1) I am happy to go to stage 2 but we need to jointly agree the details
2) I am happy to go to stage 2 but I want somebody else to suggest the details
3) I am willing to go to stage 2 but I need to see the details and I am sceptical
4) I don't think we should continue this discussion, I'm not willing to go to stage 2

What were the responses?

Q1 - Transparency of Company Figures

Everybody happy, except three colleagues who wanted somebody else to work out the details.

Q2 - Responsibility

Everybody happy, except two colleagues who were sceptical

Q3 - Choosing of Salary

A third of the company are sceptical about choosing their salaries and one person wanted somebody else to work out the details

Q4 - Transparency of Salaries

Twenty per cent of employees were sceptical and one person wanted someone else to work out the details.

I was relieved that nobody was against the whole concept, but a couple of things surprised me. Firstly, more people were sceptical about choosing their own salary than being able to see all salaries. Secondly, some people were happy to let others decide how to structure the way we work. I will need to point out that they will not be in a position to complain if they don't like the way things end up.

This brings up an interesting question as to how much control people want in their own life. Clearly some people would prefer not to have to take major decisions in their work life or their home life. This must be respected as part of a self-management philosophy, and it is vital that people be allowed to bypass a decision if it is going to cause an unnecessary level of stress.

THE INITIAL PROPOSALS – (WEEK 9)

Wait, wait. Again, rather optimistically I thought that I would be flooded with a deluge of proposals as to how people want to see things in the future.

Nothing.

At the same time, my elderly mother caught an infection and moved to a care home (I hope temporarily) for recuperation. With no proposals to read, I spent many hours with her in the home with other elderly people. Which gave me time to observe. And be impressed.

I haven't spent much time around caring professionals, and the dedication shown by the nurses and assistants was truly impressive – especially as some of the residents in the care home were not always polite or aware of their circumstances. So, I started asking questions as to how they work and why the staff seemed so motivated.

As a privately-owned company, the care home may have some similarities to Buurtzorg,[ii] the Dutch company cited as a case study in Frederic Laloux's book *Reinventing Organisations*.[iii] Their success was largely down to allowing the nurses to decide the individual care required rather than care by targets.

Lunchtime in the care home is manic. Thirty residents, fifteen staff – with no apparent order. Some people eating in chairs, some in the dining area, some in the bedrooms; many residents can eat on their own but some need help. There appears to be no specific roles or direction to staff as to who should do what. So, I asked how it worked.

No roles, just tasks given in a ten-minute morning meeting. Then the staff worked together without management interference (it was only by asking that I found out who was the senior nurse giving out the tasks), all the residents were cared for and nobody was left unfed. No paperwork, no checklists to be filled out at the time, no time spent on unnecessary tasks.

On one hand you could say that I am simplifying the work that goes into running a care home (and I am sure I am), but in terms of the front-end customer care, it was a lesson from which I felt our company, and others, could learn.

FIRST DRAFT PROPOSAL – (WEEK 10)

With a lack of proposals from others, I had little choice but to push forward with setting out my own ideas and hoping that other people would take my lead.

However, it was clear that a negative feeling was brewing about this process and some of the changes I was suggesting. The main concern appears to be a concern that the objective of the process is to reduce salaries. I felt stuck between a rock and a hard place as I didn't want to get involved in the everyday conversations (as it would then appear that I was trying to force my views) but, on the other hand, my words were being taken out of context and it seemed that the worst was being assumed.

I ploughed on and sent my colleagues a proposal which I had created using a mixture of my own methodologies with those of Frederic Laloux and Ricardo Semler.

ACCEPTING THE COLD SHOULDER – (WEEK 11)

Last week I sent out the initial proposal, hoping that there would be other proposals submitted by colleagues at the same time. This was not the case.

So, I met my own deadline of Wednesday evening for submitting proposals and wandered innocently into the office on Thursday morning.

Let us just say the atmosphere was icy! Those who had already arrived in the office were discussing my ideas. As more people arrived, the meeting got larger until I suggested that everybody disappear to the meeting room and I would handle the phones. I felt it was important that I wasn't involved in the meeting.

One lesson I was learning through this process is that often people won't do anything until forced. By providing a proposal (that they didn't like), I forced them to try to find an alternative.

What was clear, though, was that the main area of concern was related to pay and transparency. I was confused as to why this was such an issue when I was suggesting that everybody choose their own salary. In order to get people on board with the changes I want to implement, I need to get to the bottom of this.

By lunchtime it appeared that the fifteen or so people in the meeting had come up with a framework that they felt could work.

Our monthly meeting seemed a good opportunity for those who had been involved in the 'alternative proposal' process to present their recommendations to the rest of the company.

These centred around rewarding employees for various aspects of their job, including

1) The location of the employee
2) The number of years of service in the company
3) The level of stress within the job
4) The amount of travel required

It seemed to me that this proposal was similar to trying to determine pay scales in governmental organisations. My issue with this is that pay is set on specific criteria that may or may not be relevant to the company's success. Either way, I was pleased that everybody had got involved in thinking about what they wanted. Now they need to work out the details. For example, *Who defines stress? Is a particular job always stressful or only sometimes? Should those who thrive on stress receive more?*

CONFRONTING THE REAL PROBLEM – (WEEK 12)

Last week I left a group of employees to formulate their own proposal around a future pay structure. Due to the size of the first meeting, they have decided to appoint a representative from each department to work out the details and present a proposal reached by consensus.

I decided not to become involved in this, which was difficult because I felt strongly that the purpose of this change was being lost in the politics of pay scales, and people were losing sight of the main goal – namely to empower each person to take ownership of their work and the company as a whole. I was frustrated to see that transparency and choosing salaries were being seen as the goal.

The meeting didn't go well. "We seem to have gone backwards" was the overarching sentiment. What had come out of the meeting was a deeper understanding that people's priorities differ depending upon the stage of their career. What an established professional with children wants is a very different level of stability than that of a young person starting their career.

I decided not to try and sway the conversation, but it was becoming clear that the ongoing uncertainty and internal conversations were causing a lot of unrest, rumours of lower salaries and general negative feelings.

What I did want to do was to get to the bottom of why my proposal was seen as negative. So we undertook another anonymous survey asking for feelings towards each area of the proposal that I set out a couple of weeks ago. Overall most of the proposal was acceptable. However, about one third of the employees had an issue with the pay structure.

At this point, I spoke to a few people in an informal environment to try and gain a better understanding of why this was. It came down to two issues:

1) Change. People don't want to change. Whilst a few people complained about their pay, the majority were happy – so why change?

2) There is a good atmosphere in the office; there is nervousness about this changing if people know each other's salaries.

With the (I hope temporary) negativity in the office, I really hope that the team will pull a rabbit out of a hat and find a solution that they are happy with.

Chapter 8

BUILDING THE WEIRD POD WORLD

"The secret of change is to focus your energy not on fighting the old, but on building the new."
Socrates

During the first three months of our change process, much discussion and argument had taken place. The blogs in this chapter cover the subsequent three months and how, collectively, we agreed to structure the company for the future.

LIGHT AT THE END OF THE TUNNEL – (WEEK 13)

Oh! The damage a few words can do.

One of my junior colleagues sent out an email showing great enthusiasm to push the conversation forward. At last, I thought, somebody was willing to get involved. So, I congratulated him, talked to a few people who were likewise pleased by his email and thought nothing more of it.

A few days later, I was chatting with one of my senior colleagues who was furious, both with me and the author of the email. The email had clearly been understood by some very differently to the way in which I had read it. As a result, my congratulations were seen as my approval that people who had been in the company for a longer period of time would see a salary reduction.

At this point, I suggested that the conflict process should be invoked and that a direct conversation was required between those who felt aggrieved and the author of the email. So, they talked and understood what each was trying to say. The power of words!

At the same time, I had a meeting with my mentor who had (at my suggestion) been approached by people in the organisation as an anonymous sounding board. His view was that the whole process was damaging the organisation and that I should close it down and move on as it was affecting people's trust in me and the company. I was extremely opposed to doing this – the whole exercise would have been futile and, worse, the bad atmosphere in the company would continue as people would feel that their views had been sought and then ignored. Furthermore, I felt that the people who had approached him (although I didn't know who they were) were frustrated by the situation but too focused on pay alone to appreciate the bigger picture.

I decided that by the end of the week, there were going to be some workable solutions on the table one way or another. The first thing I did was something I should have done two weeks ago; I started talking to people directly. It soon became clear that the objections being voiced were more about perception than reality. A light bulb moment arose when I mentioned in passing that it is impossible for me to lower anybody's salary if they choose it. I also pointed out that it is impossible to make investment decisions (like hiring a new person) without taking into account the cost of that person.

So, the next step was to ask everybody who had ideas to voice them. Four groups formed with different proposals, so I asked them each to pick a representative. I also asked one other person, with more life experience and a different viewpoint to the rest of us, to join. My aim was to get all the ideas aired and objections out early.

I made it clear that, at this point in the process, I was taking advice, but at the end of the day the decision would be mine.

Off to the cafe and nobody leaves until the white smoke appears from the Vatican.

GETTING TO A WORKABLE SOLUTION – (WEEKS 14 and 15)

Sitting down with a fairly random group of employees, trying to find a decision that could please everybody, it appeared that some fairly interesting groups had developed:

1) *The techies* – mainly Spanish, who were already used to sharing salary information between each other;

2) *The newbies* – different nationalities, bonded by being relatively new to the company, and thus not having gained the bonuses that longer standing employees were enjoying;

3) *The oldies* (they liked to think of themselves as experienced) – needing more security of salaries;

4) *The younguns* – Americans and Northern Europeans, who had little in the way of commitments and focused on the benefits that younger workers expect;

5) *The WEIRDists* – myself, our US CEO and a few others.

With the proposals now on the table, and the clock ticking, it was imperative to keep the momentum running and find a solution that people could accept.

As the majority of employees (except the newbies) were in favour of choosing their own salary, that seemed to be an obvious first step. The tricky part was transparency. We finally agreed that each person could decide whether or not to show their salary. The salaries of those who chose not to were amalgamated and the average shown. This will probably be a minority of salaries, so at some point, confidentiality is going to become impossible as more people decide to be transparent.

The object of transparency in salaries is to allow peer pressure to ensure that people are reasonable when choosing their salaries. For those who don't want transparency, it was agreed that they could choose their own salary but the HR Director and myself would have the right to veto it.

Then came the conversation about how the bonus pot should be divided. Initially we couldn't reach an agreement on how this should be divided. However, one of the Business Development team pointed out that as we provide an ongoing service, the support, development and marketing is just as important as the sale – so the only fair way is to divide it equally, which was agreed.

But when do we pay a bonus? I took a unilateral decision on this and decided that any additional bonus should not be paid until the amount available for reinvestment (in cash, after director loan repayments, charity contributions etc. had been dealt with) was more than 15% of gross profit. Only then would 25% of the net profit be available for additional bonuses.

So, the final proposal was set out. Now all we need to do is implement it and change if required. Easy!

EXPLAINING RE-INVESTMENT – (WEEK 16)

With the final proposal in place (or at least a working methodology on which we can improve), I now need to concentrate on getting people to understand and use our new methodology.

Through this process, on numerous occasions I have felt that the need for change was still not fully understood. Although it was partly to maximise the use of each brain within the organisation, by providing the freedom and an environment in which people can soar, it was also to enhance an understanding of the company's financial situation so that employees can see the need for re-investment and make investment decisions in their day-to-day work.

Each month we hold a 90-minute meeting involving the whole company to review our financials, KPIs, previous activities and next month's goals. I felt this was a good opportunity to explain (again!) why we needed to put more money into re-investment rather than salaries. Whilst people want to know what the revenue and gross profit is, all the other figures are well …. boring. So, I put together a spreadsheet that would get me immediately thrown out of any accountancy or bookkeeping company, which butchered a profit and loss statement by adding cash items within it.

The first item shown was

Gross profit less expenses, NOT including pay.

Then I showed the amount spent on salaries and bonuses.

I wanted everybody to see the amount we were paying out in salaries and bonuses and how much profit remained – theoretically the net profit.

But then I showed the figures that aren't added into the net profit: loan repayments to directors and/or external lenders, loans to subsidiary companies (in start-up phase), charity payments, dividends, share repurchases etc.

What was a reasonable net profit suddenly seemed less positive, especially when I added a last line:

Actual amount available for re-investment

The response after the presentation was *"Why didn't you show that before? If you had shown that at the beginning it would have been clearer why we needed to change."*

Why indeed?

But will people remember this sheet when it comes to choosing salaries? It has been added on the intranet, so all I can do is to keep reminding people to look at it.

SHOWING SALARIES – (WEEK 17)

Having set out the proposals, the moment of truth had arrived – who was willing to be transparent?

Both our HR Director and I were determined not to put pressure on anybody to reveal their salary if they didn't want to. We had set our example by making the rest of the financial information transparent as well as my earnings, so now we just had to wait.

In the end, with the exception of two people, everybody chose to be transparent about their salary.

So why not the last two? I'm not entirely sure I understand their motivation but it seemed to be their view that people would perceive them for their salary rather than themselves. I don't agree, but I need to respect their decision.

With only two people choosing not to reveal their salaries, it did make me wonder why there was so much initial resistance. However, on reflection, without that pain I do not believe that people would have understood or agreed to transparency.

After going through the legal requirements we presented all salaries (with the two exceptions) at the next monthly meeting.

Our HR Director was curious to see if transparency would create what some people feared: a negative environment and mistrust amongst peers. None of this happened. On the contrary, miraculously almost all the rumours and gossip regarding salaries disappeared and you could feel the sense of relief in the air...

MANAGERS – (WEEK 20)

"You want everybody to be self-managing – right?"

"Yes."

"If you have no managers then you are going to lose a lot of people."

"I never said I don't want managers."

"But you are implementing self-management."

This conversation with my mentor sums up why it is dangerous to put a label on an idea. A number of times over the last weeks, I have had to reiterate that we need to implement our own methodology, not what somebody else has done elsewhere.

I want each person to make their own decisions (after seeking advice not consensus) about the work that they are doing. So why do we need to keep managers?

I think that managers have an important part to play in encouraging people forward, liaising between departments and developing structure and frameworks in which other people can soar. What they mustn't do is obstruct their colleagues, especially when that colleague knows more than them on a particular issue, task or project. They should often be asked for advice but should avoid making decisions.

THE FIRST EVALUATION – (WEEK 21)

The evaluation process implemented to help each person choose their own salary, included two questions:

1) How do you rate each other person in the company (weight rating from 1–5)

2) What value do you think they bring to the company (value score from 1–5)

We also asked colleagues to leave anonymous comments about their colleagues and to answer questions about their own performance.

So how did it go?

It was much quicker and easier to complete than expected. And all the scores were above 70%. This meant that a score of 70% or less indicated that there could be an issue with the way that the person is working. What will interest me more than the actual scores, is the progression of scores for each individual.

What was disappointing was that, despite being anonymous, my personal scores were initially some of the best. I do not believe that I do my job better than my colleagues. However, people will say what they think the boss wants to hear, so I need to find a way to break this. Over subsequent evaluations my score reduced, which indicates that people are becoming more honest – or I am doing worse a worse job).

I am wondering whether we should make everybody's score transparent. On one side, it allows people see how everybody is doing; on the other side, this could create an unhealthy sense of competition. On the surface this seems absurd as the scores are used only as guidance for each person to view their own performance. If somebody has a poor score, they should understand that it is not the right time to take a pay rise – and others will see that as well.

Leaving the scores aside, what about the comments? Feedback on the evaluation process suggests a mixed reaction. On the whole positive – the evaluation process provides a platform for receiving (hopefully) constructive criticism or compliments. However, the comments were mostly about how the person works rather than about the work; as a result, the comments could get personal – which could be dangerous.

We need to find a way to encourage comments to be less personal and more related to tasks undertaken etc. However, this is difficult as by doing so it will become clear who made the comment and the advantage of anonymity is lost.

Finally, what about the self-evaluation comments made by each person? No idea. These have been made anonymously, so only the HR Director and the person who made them have access to these. But hopefully they will be helpful in quarterly reviews.

We clearly have some improvements to make to this evaluation process. Not everybody will be happy with the process, but hopefully we will begin to see its value and it will provide a useful mechanism for peer feedback.

Footnote 1: After a few evaluations, we suggested that comments should be made with an owner. However, we left an option for comments to be made anonymously if required. We also decided that comments would be reviewed by the HR Director prior to distribution to allow for context to be added where required.

Footnote 2: My scores have continued to fall.

THE FIRST CHOSEN SALARIES – (WEEK 22)

With existing salaries transparent and each person provided with their evaluation results, details of comparable salaries, profit and investment statements for the company, it's now up to each person to decide their salary.

One of the adjustments that we said that everybody could make this time only was to move some of their previous bonuses into salary. This was important as some of the longer-term employees had a very low base salary, but high bonus each month.

So, what happened?

Not much.

A few people changed their entire bonus to salary. In line with the advisory process, our HR Director suggested that they may want to think whether to move some rather than all of the bonus as it would be out of line with their colleagues – some took the suggestion, some didn't. A few people increased their salary.

After making the new salaries transparent, a few people commented on some of the rises and life goes on as before.

Or does it?

The problem with being a CEO is that there is a tendency for people to tell you only what you want to hear. Perhaps some souls are more troubled than it appears about the evaluation and salary process. However, transparent salaries are vital to allow self-management to flourish – so for now I have to assume the best.

Either way, implementing our version of self-management is going to be a constant evolution – there certainly won't be a point at which point we can say "Right, done that. What's next?"

Footnote: One of the issues with fixed salaries is that there is no mechanism to provide one-off bonuses. This can mean that salaries are often increased to deal with a one-off result. I intend to add a structure where people can choose to pay themselves or a group of people a one-off bonus once a quarter if they have done something to generate a substantially higher profit for the company.

TEAL TO WEIRD AND ON – (WEEK 26)

When we first started Pod Group's change, I had no idea how long the process would take.

And I still don't.

As mentioned earlier, the inspiration for the change to self-management was Ricardo Semler. Many of the examples of what we could do came from Frederic Laloux's book *Reinventing Organisations* and his emphasis on 'Teal' organisations. However, we realised (as should any organisation) that we needed our own methodology, which we built around the characteristics of WEIRD (Wisdom, Emotional Intelligence, Initiative, Responsibility and (self) Development).

We will be evolving constantly as new employees join, as market pressures exert their force, as profits rise and fall and as new ideas are implemented.

However, in an organisation of around 50 people, with a reasonably forward-thinking workforce, six to twelve months seems like a good goal for implementing the main principles set out in our WEIRD 1.0 process. I originally thought this would be done in a couple of months but had to re-evaluate once I realised that people needed time to get comfortable with the idea.

The hardest part was, and still is, getting people interested in the finances of the company and willing to say, "this is relevant to me". I see progress, but I know that we still have a long way to go before I can extract opinions on the financial state of the company from everybody. Only when everybody understands and thinks that they have a direct influence on the financials of the company will I say that we are truly a WEIRD organisation.

However, we have started our own journey and our version of WEIRD will be exactly that – ours. Others need to follow their particular journey as there is no prescriptive formula for the future.

The next step of our journey (WEIRD 2.0) is covered in the next chapter.

Chapter 9

ACTING WEIRD

"However beautiful the strategy, you should occasionally look at the results"
Sir Winston Churchill

A) POD AND WEIRD

"If you're always trying to be normal, you will never know how amazing you can be."
Maya Angelou – American poet

Our WEIRD journey is exactly that – a journey. What started off as a vague goal to make the use of each unique brain within the company has now become a way of working (and perhaps a way of living) for us. WEIRD is not for everyone, and those who like to micro-manage and be micro-managed have a hard time adjusting to it.

It is impossible to predict the best time to push change and when to wait until everybody has digested the concept. As a result, there are no hard and fast rules on how and when to implement WEIRD practices. This can result in frustration for employees, especially those that are used to planning everything.

Self-management along the lines of WEIRD is not going to work for the majority of companies. Unless it is implemented in full, self-management is a dangerous can of worms to open. Giving people the illusion of self-management whilst not allowing it in reality will only lead to frustration and disappointment and eventually to the departure of good employees.

However, for us it has been an exciting journey. From an initial idea backed up by researching what other companies have undertaken, it took a while for everybody to see the possibilities. There followed three months of discussions and pain to reach a point where each employee felt comfortable, another month agreeing on how WEIRD would work for our company and a further two months implementing the first changes.

That was WEIRD 1.0. After this, although we had the tools in place to encourage WEIRD practices, we weren't really working in a WEIRD way as we still had departments and department heads to whom people tended to turn rather than take decisions themselves. It took another year of encouraging employees to take their own decisions before it became clear to everybody that our structure was limiting our decision-making practices (which made it easier to justify the need for further change).

Hence, we started to implement WEIRD 2.0, whereby projects, products or markets replace departments. We have deliberately avoided confining ourselves to just one of these words as we don't want to limit what any employee wants to change or start ('units' is the nearest catch-all we have got to).

So, each 'unit' is either a part of our core product that we have split up into smaller parts to target different geographical and vertical markets, or a project.

Each of these 'units' has been suggested by an employee who has taken the coordination role. At any point, any employee can suggest the need to make a new 'unit'. The coordinators then ask for volunteers to join the 'unit', thus making multi-disciplinary teams. These volunteers are free to move in and out of 'units' according to the expertise mix required. If there are no volunteers for a new 'unit' – then clearly others do not see the need for it and it will die a natural death or be revitalised at another time.

To help employees decide whether they think a 'unit' is worthwhile and therefore worth joining, we have created a template (mini-business plan) that each coordinator needs to fill in at the time of suggesting the 'unit'. This details the work required, how it will be divided, the resources and tools required and, most importantly, the budget and forecasts. Until the 'unit' is resourced with the required expertise (ie those with the relevant experience have volunteered or resources have been sourced externally), the budget will not be allocated.

With WEIRD 2.0, we have made a major structural change to create an environment that allows employees to feel in control of their working lives. Thereafter, it is necessary to watch carefully that bureaucratic processes don't slip back in.

This happened at AES, which had a self-managing organisation of over 40,000 employees running energy plants worldwide. Decisions were made at a local level every day and employees undertook multiple roles – and it was a stunningly successful company. However, with the introduction of a new CEO in 2011, the company decided that they would save money by centralising many activities at head office. A cursory look at the company's revenue, profit and share price before and after this change suggests that reverting to a hierarchical structure hasn't worked so well for AES.

To avoid this within our company, I have set a clear question for myself: as CEO, do I have any more power than anybody else to make a decision? Whilst the 'units' that I volunteer to join may be of a more general nature than some others, in terms of decision-making, I have to follow the same process as others and cannot overrule others just because I think something is a bad idea.

Every now and then I overstep the mark, but I am pleased that my colleagues now tell me when I am doing so, and I step back.

I enjoy working for the company more than I ever have; I see more potential for the company than ever and I know that my colleagues will do their best for themselves and therefore for the company. Most of all, I have shared the responsibility of the company with my colleagues and thus feel part of a team rather than fulfilling the isolated role of a traditional CEO. Finally, I have stopped trying to be the hardest working hero and have realised that I cannot control everything. I get to spend more time with my family and have a much better work–life balance. I highly recommend it.

Through the course of our change to WEIRD, we have focused on some of the 'soft' factors required to build a company that we are happy to work within. The first of these is to be authentic – for people to feel that they can manage themselves, they need to know the nature of the organisation that they represent.

B) AUTHENTICALLY WEIRD

"Be yourself, everyone else is taken."
Oscar Wilde – writer

Start-up companies often slip into the trap of trying to convey an image of a reliable company that won't be disappearing tomorrow - pretending to be larger than they are.

We have made the same mistake in the past, but I now realise that our most loyal customers don't stay with us because we have been around for nearly twenty years – but because they like what we do.

Until recently we included mission and vision statements on our website. These were lofty ideas of what we wanted to do for our customers and within our industry. However, they did not reflect what our employees wanted from work and didn't feel authentic. As a result, we removed them and now explain who we are and the values that are important to us as a team. If a customer understands our business philosophy, then great – if not, I would question whether they will understand or appreciate the service and experience that we want to give.

So how does a company be authentic? Employees must be encouraged to be themselves at work. The easiest way to encourage this is, as always, for the CEO to set an example.

Unfortunately (for the CEO), this requires opening up probably more than most CEOs would be comfortable with. CEOs are meant to have answers and make the right decisions. Being authentic includes admitting when you don't know the answer, which is surprisingly liberating. One of the roles of the CEO is to keep spirits up when things are not going well. However, this can easily slip into making overly positive statements which may reflect a best-case, rather than realistic, likelihood and come back to haunt the CEO as employees question whether statements can be relied upon going forward.

If you do get it wrong – it is better to admit it. Last year, I wasn't convinced that a new Business Development recruit was sufficiently experienced to be working with some of our existing customers. I was corrected by her colleagues and watched her in action thereafter. I was clearly wrong and apologised that I had doubted her earlier. She was surprised because she had never previously had a boss who would have admitted to such a mistake. By admitting I was wrong, I hoped that she understood that authenticity was more important than pride – and despite coming from a sales background, I have subsequently heard her admitting to customers that she doesn't know the answer to their question – thus portraying an image of authenticity to our customers.

For other people to appreciate authenticity, it is necessary to be consistent, not withholding information some of the time and being transparent at others. This gives the impression that information is being disclosed selectively. People are naturally suspicious of those that hold economic power over them – therefore being honest and consistent is vital. The easiest way to do this is to focus on the small things; be consistent with these, and employees will give their trust on the larger issues.

As an Englishman, it is part of my heritage to be self-deprecating. Again, so long as it is authentic and not an act, not taking yourself too seriously and not practising self-promotion are useful skills. Each individual should be respected for who they are, not for who they think they ought to be.

So apart from setting an example, how else can CEOs promote authenticity within a company? The easiest way is to hire authentic people. I was reading about one CEO who focuses on hiring nice people. His point was that they will be kind to your customers, who reward them with their loyalty. 'Nice' does not necessarily reflect authenticity – but it is a good start.

The next challenge is to impart a company's authenticity to the outside world. The telling of stories is a powerful method of building empathy with customers (and employees). With the amount of data fired at us every day, we are naturally sceptical. As a result, we are unlikely to view advertising positively but may be more open towards a company with a story that resonates with us. However, this needs to reflect the values of the organisation. Buffer sells a story of a transparent company that can be trusted. A cursory glance at their website tells you this is authentic – its salaries are public and available for anyone to see. The way in which they price their products and the code they use are on their website – even the books that Buffer employees are reading. For developers who value open source code and communities, for marketing people who like to know how their money is spent, for workers who long for transparency and honesty around salaries – Buffer is an organisation where they feel there are shared values. Hence consumers are willing to pay for the services that Buffer offers.

Authenticity requires listening to, and understanding, the needs of employees, suppliers and customers. However, luck can always play a part.

So can you prepare for good, or bad, luck?

C) LUCK AND PREPARATION

"Luck is what happens when preparation meets opportunity."

Seneca – Roman Philosopher

Richard Wiseman, a professor of psychology at Hertfordshire University and bestselling author, has spent many years evaluating the role of luck in people's lives. In one experiment, he compared those who described themselves as lucky to those who thought of themselves as unlucky. Both groups were asked to count the number of photographs in a newspaper. However, on page 2 in bold letters was written "Stop counting – there are 43 photographs in this newspaper." What Wiseman found was that those who described themselves as lucky were far more likely to find this message.[i]

After many such experiments Wiseman concluded that luck comes down to attitude. 'Lucky' people are more open, which leads them to grab opportunities when they arise and not get stuck when a setback hits. Contrarily, negative people create a self-fulfilling prophecy where negativity (and lack of openness) ensures that luck passes them by. This is especially true in regard to business networking – which is where a chance encounter can create business opportunities that can occasionally propel any company beyond even an optimist entrepreneur's wildest dreams.

In his book *The Virgin Way*, Richard Branson describes how Virgin Records' first album release - *Tubular Bells* by Mike Oldfield (which eventually went on to become the third biggest selling album in the 1970s) gave a kick-start to the Virgin Group. So why was Richard Branson lucky? He was trying to persuade the head of Atlantic Records to release the album in the United States. One day the movie director William Friedkin walked into Atlantic Records looking for some backing music for his new film – and Tubular Bells was playing. Friedkin used parts of the album for his film *The*

Exorcist – one of the biggest box office hits of the time. Interestingly, Branson dismisses this as 'luck', but instead hints at his tenacity.

However, tenacity isn't everything. Being born in the right country is a good start – unsurprisingly half of the difference in income worldwide is dependent on where you live. But even your name can have an influence. If you want to be an academic, a surname that starts with a letter earlier in the alphabet is more likely to result in tenure. Likewise, people with easy to pronounce names are judged more positively than those with complicated surnames. And what about the month of birth? The number of CEOs born in June and July is smaller than those born in other months. Having been born in July with a complicated surname near the end of the alphabet, I am clearly born to be weird.[ii]

Luck can even improve your health. Robert Emmons of the University of California and Michael McCullough of the University of Miami undertook an experiment in which three groups were asked to keep diaries.[iii] The first group recorded events that made them feel grateful; the second group things that irritated them and the third included both. After 10 weeks, the second two groups noted no change in their well-being. However, the first group had less frequent and less severe aches and pains, and improved sleep quality. They also felt more outgoing and compassionate, less lonely and isolated, and were happier and more alert.

So, where does luck fit into implementing WEIRD? It is necessary to provide an environment within which we are able to take advantage of opportunities when they arise.

At times, this can accelerate change. Recently, as a result of our growth, a number of communication issues have arisen within the company. This allowed me to argue that a move away from departments to units (as described earlier) would improve communication. Because people were in the right frame of mind, the next stage of our change process came about sooner than I had originally envisaged.

The hardest part about any change process is getting other people to catch up with your thought process as to why change is required. Those who understand and agree can act as advocates (or at least positive sounding boards). Finding these colleagues, and taking time to explain to them what you are trying to achieve, is vital. They don't have to be senior, but their opinions do need to be respected by others.

Business is uncertain. Positive or negative factors can arise at any time during the process of change. So, although we must always be prepared to take advantage of opportunities, we must also be willing to put things on hold if the timing is wrong.

A company culture is like an organism – it is continuously evolving and requires constant nurturing by taking advantage of the opportunities that arise while being careful not to undo the company's culture and values if bad luck hits and the company is struggling.

D) CULTURE AND VALUES

"Why is culture so important to a business? Here is a simple way to frame it. The stronger the culture, the less corporate process a company needs. When the culture is strong, you can trust everyone to do the right thing."
Brian Chesky – Airbnb CEO

This quote is particularly relevant for a company pushing a self-management culture, which depends upon the CEO's actions, rather than words.

A company's values form the basis for its culture, and each employee needs to understand what these are before any mission or vision statement can be formulated. The surest way of understanding the values of a company is to ask employees. We did this recently by asking our employees to submit their top three perceived values. These were: 1) Trust, responsibility and openness 2) Freedom and flexibility with respect to work times, location and dress code; and 3) Team.

These happen to be our values. Each company will have different values, but there are a number of steps that can be taken to guarantee an authentic culture.

The recruitment process is a vital step – employing people who fit the culture is essential. This doesn't mean that all employees should have similar characters and personalities, but rather individuals who share the same core values as that of the company, and therefore by extension other colleagues. There should be a number of interview questions aimed at assessing whether potential employees fit the company culture – these can be more important than the skills that any individual brings to the company. Our HR Director places a quote from Peter Schultz at the bottom of his email signature: "Hire character. Train skill".

However, regardless of each individual's character or the unique culture of each organisation, a few key factors are always pertinent. The first is that everybody joining Pod Group must understand the need for respecting others (a certain degree of humility is helpful here). A simple guide is that each person should treat others as they would wish to be treated. Similarly, caring about others is required to build trust and engender teamwork. After all why would you trust somebody if you know they don't care about you?

A third requirement is honesty. A lie (or even an exaggerated truth) can undo a company culture faster than anything else. Culture is rather like a reputation – it can take years to build but only a few minutes to destroy. A transparent culture facilitates honesty – as nothing needs to be hidden. This in turn improves communication.

Building a culture is, of course, about much more than just values – but without each person living the values of the organisation each day, the organisation will be built on a foundation of sand.

Having established those values, the CEO then needs to trust others to carry the organisation forward.

E) LEARNING TO TRUST

"The best way to find out if you can trust somebody is to trust them."
Ernest Hemingway – writer

Trust is two sides of the same coin.

Within a company, trust must come from the CEO and management to the employees. Specifically, they should allow employees to make the decisions they see fit without contradiction or control.

The other side of the trust coin is harder to obtain – as it is in the gift of the employees; namely that the employees trust the CEO and the management.

Ricardo Semler in conversation with Tim Ferriss talks about the creation of trust in the early days in his change to a self-management company.

His company used circuit boards that included silver on the boards. The problem was that, despite limited access and a sign in/sign out process, theft of these boards was high. Semler removed the need for signing in and singing out and thefts went up. So, he removed the lock on the door and thefts increased still further.

However, after a couple of weeks the level of thefts dropped.

Two different aspects of human psyche can be learnt from this example. Firstly, if you show people trust, generally they will repay that trust. Secondly, most people want to do the best they can at work.

By removing security on the stockroom, Semler said "I trust you". In return, most employees returned that trust. Those that carried on stealing were pushed out by colleagues who wanted to do a good job but were prevented from doing so because the materials they needed were being stolen.

The political and security climate around the world at the moment is creating an environment where the assumption of innocent until proven guilty is being reversed. I have no idea how to resolve this at a societal level beyond trying to set an example, but at a company level, CEOs and managers should actively resist punishing 98% of employees due to the actions of 2%. Punishing in this case means enacting rules, processes and procedures, pushing decision-making up the hierarchy and removing the ability for employees to take initiative and ownership of their work.

The assumption of trust on the part of CEOs can be summarised easily. They should assume that people are inherently good, can be trusted and will do their best to do the right thing. As long as a CEO believes this, then trust can be given. If at any point the CEO does not believe this – there is no point starting or continuing with a WEIRD process.

But trust needs to flow the other way as well. So how does a manager or CEO earn the trust of the employees? Part of the answer lies in showing trust first, and another part relies in showing that there is no hidden (selfish) agenda by the CEO. However, there is more.

When implementing change, the temptation is to set out a schedule for the process. However this would be a mistake because the timings will depend upon how the process evolves. Several times I have had to explain to frustrated employees that, although they think we should move forward faster, not everybody agrees and other people need more time for their thoughts to mature. It is important therefore not to make deadlines which may be missed – this will erode trust.

The timing of any change process will always be difficult when there is a business to maintain. However, undertaking the process when good news (and profits) are high makes it easier as people are confident, not worried about their jobs and less likely to resort to old practices (the true test comes when things are not so good).

It is necessary to build up a bank of trust for when things are not going so well. At this point, the CEO may need (ironically) to be more authoritarian to stop people resorting to command and control. An example of this would be to stop a manager creating a need for decisions to be passed by him or her. Keeping faith in what has been started can be testing – many will want to persuade others to transform away from the self-management practices that have been built. With a bank of trust, a CEO can keep employees on track during bad times.

Unfortunately, there will always be a minority of people who will not return trust regardless of how you treat them. Likewise, there are other people who will always assume that all business is bad, or that entrepreneurs will always maximise their personal profit at the cost of employees. So how do you treat these people?

The answer to this is easy – the same way as you treat everybody else. If they don't want to trust, that is up to them – but if they are suspicious, that won't change until you have proven your trust in them. If, however, it becomes clear that these 2% are damaging the potential of the 98% and they refuse to change, then you need to consider dismissing 2% of employees. The other 98% will thank you and feel a greater sense of ownership towards the company.

F) TREAT EVERYONE AS AN OWNER AND CEO

"A leadership culture is one where everyone thinks like an owner, a CEO or a managing director. It's one where everyone is entrepreneurial and proactive."
Robin S. Sharma – writer

I am not a fan of communism (I saw first-hand the effects of it when I lived in Russia soon after Perestroika). Forcing common ownership encourages a sense of unhealthy entitlement and ultimately demotivates those you want to motivate.

However, employee ownership promotes the type of motivation that allows employees to take control of their destinies. Telling a colleague when asked for advice, "you own part of the company, take this into account when you make your decision" has a great deal more impact on their decision-making process than "make a good decision, even though you will not gain from the additional value that you create as a result of that decision".

The amount of ownership given to employees is less important – after a certain point, giving more has no effect on motivation anyway. What is more important is how equity is split between the employees. As with salaries, the amount of equity is not necessarily the important aspect – what is key is how much each person gets compared to their peers. I found that the easiest way to facilitate the division of shares was to provide a pool of shares for employees and allow them to choose how that pool should be divided.

The other benefit of providing equity to employees is that the grass needs to be a lot greener on the other side for somebody to leave the company. Our lives have become a great deal more transient than even ten years ago. As a result, the building of a really effective team based on trust has become harder. However, providing ownership (alongside great working conditions) encourages people to stay.

Finally, ask yourself what you are really losing by giving away equity (the same question needs to be asked for giving up control). Some years ago, I got into a conversation with a friend about what amount of money constitutes success (he was already a multi-millionaire). He genuinely couldn't answer the question but instead was focused on making millions on his next venture. His boyfriend asked a more pertinent question – how much money do you need to be happy?

Not having enough money leads to stress and unhappiness. To quote Mr Micawber from Charles Dickens' play *David Copperfield*:

> *"Annual income twenty pounds, annual expenditure nineteen pounds nineteen and six, result happiness. Annual income twenty pounds, annual expenditure twenty pounds ought and six, result misery."*

But how much expenditure (when less than income) leads to happiness? My own rule of thumb is to be able to afford any reasonable purchase or activity without having to think whether it can be afforded. The word 'reasonable' is obviously open to interpretation – but choosing a standard of living – and being happy with it – is a good start.

The goal of most entrepreneurs today is to build a company that can be sold – preferably for a large sum. Which brings up the question: How much of that large sum is it necessary to keep? Ricardo Semler has a fairly easy formula which is that you need to have assets equal to twenty times your annual expenditure. Whether you take that formula or another, if you build your company successfully (which is more likely if you incentivise your employees), there is a very strong chance that you won't have any need for the equity that you gave away to your employees.

In a conversation with the CEO of one of my competitors, who had recently been bought by a private equity group, he was genuinely surprised by the amount of satisfaction he gained by sharing some of the money from the buy out with his employees. I got the feeling that the day he gave out the bonus cheques to employees was probably one of the most satisfying of his business career.

This chapter has focused on some of the soft skills that help implement an environment of WEIRD. But as with other parts of the WEIRD methodology, nothing can be prescriptive about the soft skills required. There is much more that could be written on the subject of WEIRD but, at some point, every book must come to an end.

CONCLUSION

We are facing a very uncertain world over the next 15 years.

Automation will allow industries to scale which may create new jobs in disruptive technologies, however Artificial Intelligence will destroy millions of jobs. It is unlikely that the creation of new technologies will overcome the loss of jobs – especially in the short term. Unless we change, many people will be forced to take unwanted jobs or have no employment at all. There is already a major division between the very rich and those who are struggling to survive; and there is a strong chance that the effects of Artificial Intelligence will widen this gap. Therefore, we need to look seriously at whether the Universal Basic Income is not only practical but also necessary in order to avoid civil breakdown. Employment in the future will either be oriented towards tasks that require creativity, Emotional Intelligence and initiative or the opposite – of such low value that it is not worth investing in robots or computers to undertake the work.

Despite being able to foresee these changes, our education of children is still based on the principles (and sometimes materials) of thirty years ago. Finally, social media companies such as Facebook and Twitter use envy to persuade us that we should be better versions of ourselves, which leads to stress, mental illness and other societal issues that we should be avoiding.

On the positive side, despite what the media may lead us to believe, worldwide there is less poverty than at any point in the history of man. Globally, we are safer, richer and healthier than we have ever been. Millions of people are moving from merely surviving to having (albeit limited) choices about where and how they want to live. New generations have a greater sense of their rights, money is not the key motivator and they expect their employers to act honestly – otherwise they will move elsewhere.

It is this new generation that will create the change in how we work and live – most of all by continuing to create the companies that will challenge the old way of working. Man is an innovative being, and this innovation will help us survive and thrive.

I hope, by suggesting an alternative way to deal with the future of work, that I might touch the imagination of one or two people. Many will accuse me of being at best optimistic, at worst delusional.

Perhaps they are correct. It is the right of each of us to choose how we wish to live our lives, but what I hope I have set out is a vision of alternative future of work that I firmly believe could lead to happier lives and a better world.

Good luck on your WEIRD adventure. However it turns out – it will be your journey.

If you want to know more about the WEIRD philosophy or want to contact Charles, more information can be found at www.weirdceo.com or email info@weirdceo.com.

Dedication

Sandra, Ana & Sofia – This wouldn't have happened without you.

Acknowledgements

Creating this book has ended up as a team effort, for which many thanks are due.

Amy Garcia is (I think) to be thanked for pushing me to write the book in the first place and has been a force in organising its promotion alongside David Clare and Connor Mitchell at Tyto PR. Jan Wade and Chris Cartwright have given invaluable editorial advice alongside my colleagues Sally Meadows and Ned Richards. Thank you also to Lara Marques for the cover design and graphics included within the book.

However, this book would not have come about without the willingness of my colleagues at Pod Group as we ventured into the unknown. An army officer's evaluation comes to mind – 'his men would follow him anywhere, but only out of morbid curiosity'.

Special thanks must go to Charidimos Spourdalakis who has been an inspiration and sounding board throughout the process of implementing our WEIRD methodology and has tempered some of my more insane ideas.

Finally, my biggest thanks are to my wife, Sandra, who edited the early versions; and my children who - on those occasions when I wasn't actually writing - had to listen to more about Artificial Intelligence and WEIRD than any normal person could endure.

References

Introduction

[i] Yates, E. (2017, March 25). *What Happens to Your Brain When You Get a Like on Instagram?* Retrieved from Business Insider: http://www.businessinsider.com/what-happens-to-your-brain-like-instagram-dopamine-2017-3

[ii] Refer to EY study in Chapter 4 for split between older and younger millennials.

[iii] Altan, L. (2017, November 22). *Millennials And Entitlement In The Workplace: The Good, The Bad, And The Ugly.* Retrieved from Forbes: https://www.forbes.com/sites/larryalton/2017/11/22/millennials-and-entitlement-in-the-workplace-the-good-the-bad-and-the-ugly/#4fbd1cb53943

[iv] Temin, P. ((Spring, 2004), 513–538.). *The Labor Market of the Early Roman Empire.* Retrieved from Journal of Interdisciplinary History: https://pdfs.semanticscholar.org/3378/a942f7f11d586ddffc5785c2c78f7ee71ac5.pdf

[v] Barnett, D. (2017, November 30). *The Robots Are Coming – but Will They Really Take All Our Jobs?* Retrieved from Independent: http://www.independent.co.uk/news/science/robots-are-coming-but-will-they-take-our-jobs-uk-artificial-intelligence-doctor-who-a8080501.html

References

[vi] Forbes. (2017, November 7). *The Little-Known Relationship Between Emotional Intelligence and Success.* Retrieved from https://www.forbes.com/sites/forbescoachescouncil/2017/11/07/the-little-known-relationship-between-emotional-intelligence-and-success/#2eb300d2696d

[vii] Casel. (2017, February). *To Reach the Students, Teach the Teachers.* Retrieved from http://www.casel.org/wp-content/uploads/2017/02/SEL-TEd-Executive-Summary-for-CASEL-2017-02-14.pdf

[viii] Center for Benefit-Cost Studies in Education, Columbia University. (2015, February). *The Economic Value of Social and Emotional Learning.* Retrieved from http://blogs.edweek.org/edweek/rulesforengagement/SEL-Revised.pdf

Chapter 1 – The Need To Be Weird

[i] Business Insider. (2017, August 2). *Here's Why Small Businesses Fail.* Retrieved from http://www.businessinsider.com/why-small-businesses-fail-infographic-2017-8

[ii] Urban, T. (2015, January 22). *Artificial Intelligence Revolution.* Retrieved from Waitbutwhy.com: http://waitbutwhy.com/2015/01/artificial-intelligence-revolution-1.html

[iii] Charles Lew. (2018, July 17) Artificial Intelligence And The Evolution of Law. Retrieved from https://www.forbes.com/sites/forbeslacouncil/2018/07/17/artificial-intelligence-and-the-evolution-of-law/#1219a5f236ee

[iv] Quartz. (2017, December 13). One survey conducted by Quartz last year found that 90% of respondents thought that up to half of all jobs would be lost to automation in five years, but 91% said there was "no risk to my job".

[v] Schwartz, B. (2005). *The Paradox of Choice.* TED talk. Retrieved from https://www.ted.com/talks/barry_schwartz_on_the_paradox_of_choice#t-1161114

[vi] Digital Strategies for Travel Europe 2017. (2017, November 9) The age of anxiety and why too much choice is a bad thing. Retrieved from https://www.eyefortravel.com/revenue-and-data-management/age-anxiety-and-why-too-much-choice-bad-thing

Clancy Yeates. (2018, June 5). When too much choice is a bad thing. Retrieved from https://www.smh.com.au/money/super-and-retirement/when-too-much-choice-is-a-bad-thing-20180528-p4zhyt.html

[vii] Indy Johar. (2017, July 13). *Ten Provocations for the Next 10 Years of Social Innovation.* Retrieved from https://provocations.darkmatterlabs.org/massive-change-10-provocations-for-the-next-10-years-of-social-innovation-df4756ed8629

[viii] Forbes. (2018, April 23). *Who Really Owns Your Health Data?* Retrieved from https://www.forbes.com/sites/forbestechcouncil/2018/04/23/who-really-owns-your-health-data/#614861e36d62

References

[ix] Russia Beyond. (2018, April 10). *Dos and Donts of Russian.* Retrieved from https://www.rbth.com/lifestyle/328026-dos-and-donts-of-russian

[x] Robinson, K. (2006, February). *Do Schools Kill Creativity?* TED Talk. Retrieved from https://www.ted.com/talks/ken_robinson_says_schools_kill_creativity?

[xi] Frederic Laloux. (2014, February). Reinventing Organizations. Retrieved from https://www.amazon.co.uk/Reinventing-Organizations-Creating-Inspired-Consciousness/dp/2960133501/ref=tmm_pap_swatch_0?_encoding=UTF8&qid=&sr=

[xii] statista. (2018, January). *EU Youth Unemployment.* Retrieved from https://www.statista.com/statistics/266228/youth-unemployment-rate-in-eu-countries/

[xiii] Chris Weller. (2017, May 15). Why Finland's education system puts others to shame? Retrieved from https://www.weforum.org/agenda/2017/05/why-finlands-education-system-puts-others-to-shame

[xiv] Daniel Goleman. (2005, September 27). Emotional Intelligence: Why It Can Matter More Than IQ. Retrieved from https://www.amazon.com/Emotional-Intelligence-Matter-More-Than/dp/055338371X/ref=tmm_pap_swatch_0?_encoding=UTF8&qid=1534166954&sr=8-2&dpID=51MkFTvog0L&preST=_SY291_BO1,204,203,200_QL40_&dpSrc=detail

[xv] Kinesics. Retrieved from https://en.wikipedia.org/wiki/Kinesics

[xvi] Barrett, L. F. (2017, December). *You Aren't at the Mercy of Your Emotions – Your Brain Creates Them.* TED Talk. Retrieved from https://www.ted.com/talks/lisa_feldman_barrett_you_aren_t_at_the_mercy_of_your_emotions_your_brain_creates_them

[xvii] Ricardo Semler. (2017, March 28). Leading Wisely. Retrieved from https://itunes.apple.com/us/podcast/leading-wisely/id1198783363?mt=2

[xviii] TinyPulse. (2014, November 4). *New Study Answers: What Motivates Employees To "Go The Extra Mile?"* Retrieved from https://www.forbes.com/sites/victorlipman/2014/11/04/what-motivates-employees-to-go-the-extra-mile-study-offers-surprising-answer/#1e141f65a055

Chapter 2 – Technological Change

[i] Tearle, Oliver. (2017, April 26). *A Short Analysis of William Blake's 'Jerusalem'.* Retrieved from https://interestingliterature.com/2017/04/26/a-short-analysis-of-william-blakes-jerusalem/

[i] Matthias Bruckner, Marcelo LaFleur, Ingo Pitterle. (2017). "The Impact of the Technological Revolution on Labour Markets and Income Distribution." *Frontier Magazine Digital Issues* 7. Retrieved from https://www.sentryo.net/the-4-industrial-revolutions/

[ii] Godin, Seth. (2017, May 17). *What Henry Ford understood about wages.* Retrieved from

References

http://sethgodin.typepad.com/seths_blog/2017/05/what-henry-ford-understood-about-wages.html

iii Matthias Bruckner, Marcelo LaFleur, Ingo Pitterle. (2017). "The Impact of the Technological Revolution on Labour Markets and Income Distribution." *Frontier Magazine Digital Issues* 7. Retrieved from https://www.sentryo.net/the-4-industrial-revolutions/

iv Schwab, Klaus. (2016). *Shaping the Fourth Industrial Revolution.* World Economic Forum.

v Pogue, David. (2017, May 1). *Batteries Have Gotten Better, but There's Still Room for Improvement.* Retrieved from https://www.scientificamerican.com/article/batteries-have-gotten-better-but-theres-still-room-for-improvement/

vi Santens, Scott. (2015, May 14). *Self-Driving Trucks Are Going to Hit Us Like a Human-Driven Truck.* Retrieved from https://medium.com/basic-income/self-driving-trucks-are-going-to-hit-us-like-a-human-driven-truck-b8507d9c5961

vii LA Times. (2016, January 5). Retrieved from http://www.latimes.com/business/technology/la-fi-0105-lyft-growth-20160105-story.html

viii Statista. (2018, February). Retrieved from https://www.statista.com/statistics/192361/unadjusted-monthly-number-of-full-time-employees-in-the-us/

[ix] Balakrishnan, Anita. (2017, May 22). *Self-driving cars could cost America's professional drivers up to 25,000 jobs a month, Goldman Sachs says*. Retrieved from https://www.cnbc.com/2017/05/22/goldman-sachs-analysis-of-autonomous-vehicle-job-loss.html

[x] Liberatore, Stacy. (2016, September 10). *A woman in an electric wheelchair chasing a duck with a broom and people playing frogger on busy roads: Google reveals the weirdest things its self-driving car has seen*. Retrieved from http://www.dailymail.co.uk/sciencetech/article-3782569/A-woman-electric-wheelchair-chasing-duck-broom-people-playing-Frogger-naked-people-running-close-look-Google-reveals-weirdest-things-self-driving-car-seen.html

[xi] Weiland, Jeruld. (2017, February 5). *How Safe Are Self-Driving Cars?* Retrieved from https://www.huffingtonpost.com/entry/how-safe-are-self-driving-cars_us_5908ba48e4b03b105b44bc6b

[xii] Weston, Phoebe. (2017, October 9). *Humans will be BANNED from driving cars within the next 25 years as 'safer' autonomous vehicles hit the road, expert claims*. Retrieved from http://www.dailymail.co.uk/sciencetech/article-4963612/Humans-BANNED-driving-25-years.html

[xiii] Think Academy. (2014, October 7). IBM Watson: How it works. Retrieved from https://www.youtube.com/watch?time_continue=9&v=_Xcmh1LQB9I

[xiv] Maruti. Retrieved from https://www.marutitech.com/cognitive-computing-features-scope-limitations/

References

xv Roser, Max. (2016). Retrieved from
https://en.wikipedia.org/wiki/File:Moore%27s_Law_Transistor_Count_1971-2016.png

xvi Windows 1.0 required 256KB RAM. Windows 10 – 2GB

xvii Urban, Tim. (2017). Retrieved from *Neuralink and Brain's Magical Future.* https://waitbutwhy.com/2017/04/neuralink.html

xviii ScienceBlogs. (2017, March 27). *10 Important Differences Between Brains and Computers.* Retrieved from
http://scienceblogs.com/developingintelligence/2007/03/27/why-the-brain-is-not-like-a-co/

xix *Forbes. (2018, May 21). How Much Data Do We Create Every Day? The Mind-Blowing Stats Everyone Should Read. Retrieved from*
https://www.forbes.com/sites/bernardmarr/2018/05/21/how-much-data-do-we-create-every-day-the-mind-blowing-stats-everyone-should-read/#144e42160ba9

xx CoWorkr. (2017, June 2). *How new IoT hardware is supporting the growth in indoor sensing.* Retrieved from
http://coworkr.co/articles/2017/6/2/how-new-iot-hardware-is-supporting-the-growth-in-indoor-sensing

xxi Han Seung Lee, Mohamed A. Ismail, Jitendra Kumar Singh & Jun Ho Shin. (2017). "Embedded sensor system to detect chloride permeation in concrete: an overview." *The International Journal of Corrosion*

Processes and Corrosion Control 373-382. Retrieved from
http://www.tandfonline.com/doi/full/10.1080/1478422X.2017.1300218

[xxii] Jacobsen, Bruno. (2018, January 11). *The Future of Employment – 3 Things You Need to Know.* Retrieved from
https://www.futuresplatform.com/blog/future-of-employment-work-automation-artificial-intelligence-ai

[xxiii] Metz, Cade. (2015, September 7). *GOOGLE SAYS ITS AI CATCHES 99.9 PERCENT OF GMAIL SPAM.* Retrieved from
https://www.wired.com/2015/07/google-says-ai-catches-99-9-percent-gmail-spam/

[xxiv] British Medical Journal. (2017, July 3). "Can search engine data predict pancreatic cancer?" Retrieved from
http://www.bmj.com/content/358/bmj.j3159

[xxv] Strickland, Eliza. (2017, August 11). *IBM Watson Makes a Treatment Plan for Brain-Cancer Patient in 10 Minutes; Doctors Take 160 Hours.* Retrieved from https://spectrum.ieee.org/the-human-os/biomedical/diagnostics/ibm-watson-makes-treatment-plan-for-brain-cancer-patient-in-10-minutes-doctors-take-160-hours

[xxvi] Mandy, Oaklander. (2016, May 3). *Medical Errors Are the Third Leading Cause of Death: Study.* Retrieved from
http://time.com/4316818/leading-cause-of-death-medical-errors/

[xxvii] Mariusz Bojarski, B. F. (2017, August 17). *End-to-End Deep Learning for Self-Driving Cars*. Retrieved from NVIDIA Developer Web Site: https://devblogs.nvidia.com/deep-learning-self-driving-cars/

[xxviii] Riccardo Miotto, L. L. (2016). *Deep Patient: An Unsupervised Representation to Predict the Future of Patients from the Electronic Health Records*. Scientific Reports volume 6, Article number: 26094 .

[xxix] Rajnoch, D. (2017, July 23). *How does machine learning work? Like a brain!* Retrieved from Towards Data Science Web Site: https://towardsdatascience.com/how-does-machine-learning-work-a3bf1e102b11

[xxx] Masolo, C. (2017, May 07). *Supervised, unsupervised and deep learning*. Retrieved from Towards Data Science Web Site: https://towardsdatascience.com/supervised-unsupervised-and-deep-learning-aa61a0e5471c

[xxxi] Masolo, C. (2017, May 07). *Supervised, unsupervised and deep learning*. Retrieved from Towards Data Science Web Site: https://towardsdatascience.com/supervised-unsupervised-and-deep-learning-aa61a0e5471c

[xxxii] Knight, W. (2017, April 11). *The Dark Secret at the Heart of AI*. Retrieved from MIT Technology Review: https://www.technologyreview.com/s/604087/the-dark-secret-at-the-heart-of-ai/

xxxiii Towers-Clark, C. (2018, September 19). *Can we make Artificial Intelligence accountable?* Retrieved from Forbes.com: https://www.forbes.com/sites/charlestowersclark/2018/09/19/can-we-make-artificial-intelligence-accountable/#2b4e5655364e

xxxiv Horton, H. (2016, March 24). *Microsoft deletes 'teen girl' AI after it became a Hitler-loving sex robot within 24 hours.* Retrieved from The Telegraph: https://www.telegraph.co.uk/technology/2016/03/24/microsofts-teen-girl-ai-turns-into-a-hitler-loving-sex-robot-wit/

xxxv Wright, M. (2018, February 01). *It's 2018, let's talk about machine bias.* Retrieved from AI & Intelligent Automation Network: https://www.aiia.net/artificial-intelligence/articles/its-2018-lets-talk-about-machine-bias?utm_campaign=AIIA-NL-18-01-09&utm_medium=email&utm_source=internalemail&MAC=%7C1-DHXIAYB&elqContactId=2939508&disc=

xxxvi Fedak, V. (2017, September 11). *The future of AI: Deep Learning... or much more?* Retrieved from Towards Data Science: https://towardsdatascience.com/the-future-of-ai-deep-learning-or-much-more-eb95ed5da487

xxxvii PWC. (2018, February 6). "Will robots really steal our jobs?" *PWC Economics Web Site.* Retrieved from https://www.pwc.co.uk/economic-services/assets/international-impact-of-automation-feb-2018.pdf.

xxxviii Bland, Ben. (2016, June 6). *China's robot revolution.* Retrieved from https://www.ft.com/content/1dbd8c60-0cc6-11e6-ad80-67655613c2d6.

References

xxxix Urban, Tim. *The AI Revolution: The Road to Superintelligence.* Retrieved from https://waitbutwhy.com/2015/01/artificial-intelligence-revolution-1.html.

xl Urban, Tim. (2015, January 22). *The AI Revolution: The Road to Superintelligence.* Retrieved from https://waitbutwhy.com/2015/01/artificial-intelligence-revolution-1.html

xli Investors.com. (2018, February 20). *AI In Business: This Is What The Future Holds.* Retrieved from https://www.investors.com/news/technology/ai-in-business-future-of-artificial-intelligence/

xlii Teffer, Peter. (2018, February 28). *Robotics MEP angry at lack of Commission response on AI.* Retrieved from https://euobserver.com/science/141143

xliii Heller, Nathan. (2017, December 18 & 25). *Estonia, the Digital Republic.* Retrieved from https://www.newyorker.com/magazine/2017/12/18/estonia-the-digital-republic

xliv Sandle, Tim. (2017, October 1). *Is the U.K. ahead with the digitalization of healthcare?* Retrieved from http://www.digitaljournal.com/life/health/is-the-u-k-ahead-with-the-digitalization-of-healthcare/article/503922

xlv e-estonia. *Public Safety.* Retrieved from https://e-estonia.com/

[xlvi] Heller, Nathan. (2017 December 18 & 25). *Estonia, the Digital Republic.* Retrieved from
https://www.newyorker.com/magazine/2017/12/18/estonia-the-digital-republic

[xlvii] Veerpalu, Anne. (2017, September 14). *Estonian legislation history: self-driving vehicles are now regulated by law.* Retrieved from
https://www.njordlaw.com/estonian-legislation-history-self-driving-vehicles-now-regulated-law/

[xlviii] Perkins, Anne. (2018, March 6). *Government to review law before self-driving cars arrive on UK roads.* Retrieved from
https://www.theguardian.com/technology/2018/mar/06/self-driving-cars-in-uk-riding-on-legal-review

[xlix] Seba, James Arbib & Tony. (2017, May). *Rethinking Transportation 2020-2030.* Retrieved from
https://static1.squarespace.com/static/585c3439be65942f022bbf9b/t/591a2e4be6f2e1c13df930c5/1494888038959/RethinkX+Report_051517.pdf?pdf=RethinkingTransportation

[l] The Atlantic. (2017, March 30). *How Many Robots Does It Take to Replace a Human Job?* Retrieved from
https://www.theatlantic.com/business/archive/2017/03/work-automation/521364/

[li] Carl Benedikt Frey, Michael A. Osborne. (2013). *The future of employment: How susceptible are jobs to computerisation?* Oxford: Oxford Martin School – University of Oxford.

References

[iii] Autor, David H. (2015). "Why Are There Still So Many Jobs? The History and Future of Workplace Automation." *Journal of Economic Perspectives* 3-30.

Chapter 3 – Business Change

[i] New York Times. (2016, January 22). *The eight second attention span.* Retrieved from https://www.nytimes.com/2016/01/22/opinion/the-eight-second-attention-span.html?_r=0

[ii] Fast Company. (2017, March 3). *6-ways-to-become-a-better-listener.* Retrieved from https://www.fastcompany.com/3068959/6-ways-to-become-a-better-listener

[iii] HBR. (2015, February). *The art of giving and receiving advice.* Retrieved from Harvard Business Review: https://hbr.org/2015/01/the-art-of-giving-and-receiving-advice

Chapter 4 – Social Change

[i] EY. (2016). *Next-gen workforce: secret weapon or biggest challenge.* Retrieved from http://www.ey.com/Publication/vwLUAssets/ey-next-gen-workforce-secret-weapon-or-biggest-challenge/$FILE/ey-pdf-next-gen-workforce-secret-weapon-or-biggest-challenge.pdf

[ii] IFL Science. (2017, July 26). *How Much Data Does The World Generate Every Minute?* Retrieved from http://www.iflscience.com/technology/how-much-data-does-the-world-generate-every-minute/

[iii] Harari, Y. (2017). Retrieved from
http://www.ynharari.com/book/homo-deus/

[iv] School of Life. (2016). Retrieved from
https://www.youtube.com/watch?v=sPOuIyEJnbE

[v] Marr, B. (2017, August 14). *Want To Use Big Data? Why Not Start Via Google, Facebook, Amazon, (Etc.).* Retrieved from Forbes Web Site:
https://www.forbes.com/sites/bernardmarr/2017/08/14/want-to-use-big-data-why-not-start-via-google-facebook-amazon-etc/#6f20931c3d5d

[vi] Sulleyman, A. (2017, July 17). *Elon Musk: AI is a "fundamental existential risk for human civilisation" and creators must slow down.* Retrieved from Independent Web Site:
http://www.independent.co.uk/life-style/gadgets-and-tech/news/elon-musk-ai-human-civilisation-existential-risk-artificial-intelligence-creator-slow-down-tesla-a7845491.html

[vii] Future of Life Institute. (2017). *Asilomar AI Principles.* Retrieved from
https://futureoflife.org/ai-principles/

[viii] Straub, J. (2017, October 23). *Does regulating artificial intelligence save humanity or just stifle innovation?* Retrieved from The Conversation: http://theconversation.com/does-regulating-artificial-intelligence-save-humanity-or-just-stifle-innovation-85718

References

[ix] Institute for Public Policy Research (IPPR). (2017, December 28). *Managing Automation*. Retrieved from The Guardian Web Site: https://www.theguardian.com/technology/2017/dec/28/uks-poorest-to-fare-worst-in-age-of-automation-thinktank-warns

[x] Davies, H. (2017, June 21). *Why is productivity so low since the crisis – particularly in the UK?* Retrieved from The Guardian Web Site: https://www.theguardian.com/business/2017/jun/21/productivity-crisis-uk-real-wage-growth

[xi] Roosevelt Institute. (n.d.). Retrieved from https://futurism.com/experts-universal-basic-income-boost-us-economy-staggering-2-5-trillion/

[xii] Gallop. (2013, October 13). *Worldwide, 13% of Employees Are Engaged at Work.* Retrieved from http://news.gallup.com/poll/165269/worldwide-employees-engaged-work.aspx

[xiii] Telegraph. (2018, January 20). *It's official: most people are miserable at work.* Retrieved from http://www.telegraph.co.uk/finance/jobs/11871751/Its-official-most-people-are-miserable-at-work.html

[xiv] Forget, E. (2011, September). *The Town with No Poverty: The Health Effects of a Canadian Guaranteed Annual Income Field Experiment.* Retrieved from https://economics.ca//cgi/jab?journal=cpp&article=v37n3p0283

Chapter 5 – Educational Change

[i] Ferster, B. (2017, January 21). *Intelligent Tutoring Systems: What Happened?* Retrieved from https://elearningindustry.com/intelligent-tutoring-systems-what-happened

[ii] Data&Society. (2016, July 22). *Personalized Learning: The Conversation We Are Not Having*. Retrieved from https://datasociety.net/pubs/ecl/PersonalizedLearning_primer_2016.pdf

[iii] Yale Center for Emotional Intelligence. (2013, September). *Transforming Students' Lives with Social and Emotional Learning*. Retrieved from http://ei.yale.edu/wp-content/uploads/2013/09/Transforming-Students%E2%80%99-Lives-with-Social-and-Emotional-Learning.pdf

Chapter 6 – The Theory Of WEIRD

[i] Glassdoor. (2016, March 23). *Demystifying the gender pay gap*. Retrieved from https://www.glassdoor.com/research/demystifying-the-gender-pay-gap/

[ii] Academy of Management. (2017, November 30). *Signaling in Secret: Pay for Performance and the Incentive and Sorting Effects of Pay Secrecy*. Retrieved from https://journals.aom.org/doi/abs/10.5465/amj.2012.0937

[iii] Forbes. (2016, March 11). *Women consistently outperform men*. Retrieved from https://www.forbes.com/sites/victorlipman/2016/03/11/new-study-

shows-women-consistently-outperform-men-in-emotional-intelligence/#2f41a996335d

Chapter 7 – Destroying The Old Pod WEIRD

[i] http://www.ted.com/talks/dan_pink_on_motivation

[ii] http://www.buurtzorgusa.org/

[iii] http://www.reinventingorganizations.com/

Chapter 9 – Acting WEIRD

[i] Wiseman, Richard. n.d.
https://www.forbes.com/sites/forbesfinancecouncil/2018/01/02/what-is-luck-and-does-it-affect-your-chances-of-success/#119d148f1611.

[ii] Kaufman, Scott Barry. 2018. 1 March.
https://blogs.scientificamerican.com/beautiful-minds/the-role-of-luck-in-life-success-is-far-greater-than-we-realized/.

[iii] Emmons, Robert. 2003.
https://greatergood.berkeley.edu/images/application_uploads/Emmons-CountingBlessings.pdf.

CPSIA information can be obtained
at www.ICGtesting.com
Printed in the USA
BVHW071732201118
533641BV00001B/10/P